500 Classroom Tips
Preschool

M000112443

Table of Contents

500 Classroom Tips
Preschool

About This Book

Looking for creative ideas to get organized and add some fresh appeal to your classroom routines? We've got 500 of them just for you! Whether you're a first-year or seasoned teacher, this idea-packed resource is your guide to creating and maintaining a motivating and productive classroom. We've collected the best classroom-tested ideas from *The Mailbox®* magazine and conveniently organized them into one comprehensive package. Inside you'll quickly and easily find surefire suggestions on the timely topics you need most!

- Classroom Routines and Events
- Organizational Tips
- Curriculum Ties and Lesson Helps
- Arts and Crafts
- Student Motivation and Work Management
- Communication

Managing Editor: Susan Walker

Editorial Team: Becky S. Andrews, Kimberley Bruck, Karen P. Shelton, Diane Badden, Susan Walker, Kimberly A. Brugger, Karen A. Brudnak, Sarah Hamblet, Hope Rodgers, Dorothy C. McKinney

Production Team: Lisa K. Pitts, Jennifer Tipton Bennett (COVER ARTIST), Pam Crane, Clevell Harris, Rebecca Saunders, Jennifer Tipton Bennett, Chris Curry, Theresa Lewis Goode, Ivy L. Koonce, Clint Moore, Greg D. Rieves, Barry Slate, Donna K. Teal, Tazmen Carlisle, Amy Kirtley-Hill, Kristy Parton, Debbie Shoffner, Cathy Edwards Simrell, Lynette Dickerson, Mark Rainey

www.themailbox.com

Manufactured in the United States
10 9 8 7 6 5 4 3 2

Classroom Routines and Events

Contents

Squared Away With Carpet Squares

To ensure a calm start to your day, try this management technique. Before children arrive at school, place a carpet square and a book on the floor for each child. After you welcome each child, ask him to sit on the carpet square of his choice. As the children quietly browse through the provided books, you'll have a chance to get your administrative tasks all squared away.

Claudia Pinkston—Four-Year-Olds
Lexington, SC

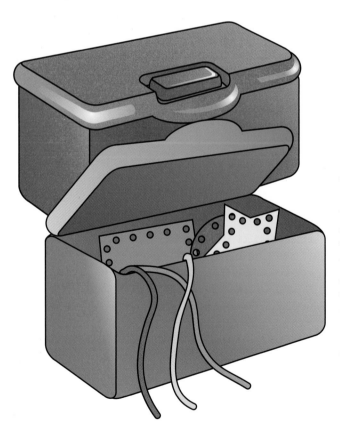

Mystery Boxes

Here's an activity that will keep little ones busy while you handle morning routines. Collect a supply of empty baby wipes boxes. Fill each box with a different set of toys such as dominoes, toy cars, or lacing cards. As children enter the room, allow them to choose a "mystery box" from a special shelf. When a child finishes with one box of toys, he may return it and take another. As children discover and play, you'll be free to take care of last-minute notes and answer parent questions.

Barbara M. Marks—PreK
Kinderplace
Oshkosh, WI

Check In

End early morning confusion with this easy management system. Personalize a library card pocket for each child and mount each pocket on a bulletin board. To make attendance cards, cut a supply of 3" x 5" construction paper cards from two contrasting colors. Pair contrasting cards, and glue them back-to-back. Label one side of each card with the word *home* and the other side with *school* and illustrate both sides. Insert a card in each pocket with the home side showing. As youngsters enter the classroom each morning, they check in by turning their cards to the school side. To check out in the afternoon, they turn their cards to the home side. With this system, you can see at a glance who is absent.

Ann Rowe—Special Education, Western Hills, Omaha Public Schools, Omaha, NE

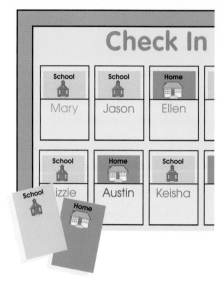

Taking Roll

To make taking attendance a simple matter and help youngsters practice name recognition, try this management aid. Personalize an apple cutout for each child. Attach a small piece of magnetic tape to the back of each cutout. On a wall, within your youngsters' reach, mount a strip of magnetic tape. Write each child's name on a small worm cutout and mount it above the strip of magnetic tape. Each morning, as each little one enters your room, have her locate her name on a worm and mount her apple on the magnetic tape below it. Change the cutouts to pumpkins and vines for October and turkeys and cornucopias for November. This quick and easy method will tell you at a glance which children are absent.

adapted from an idea by Becky Gibson, Ladonia Elementary, Auburn, AL

Seasonal Nametags

To make taking attendance a simple matter and help youngsters practice name recognition, create durable seasonal nametags. For each child, personalize a laminated seasonal cutout such as a leaf, an apple, or a pumpkin. Attach a piece of magnetic tape to the back of each cutout. Then place these nametags on a table. Draw an illustration on the board to correspond with the nametags. For example, if the nametag is an apple cutout, draw a tree outline on the blackboard. Each morning, as each student enters your room, have him locate his nametag and mount it on the blackboard illustration. Change the nametags and the illustration monthly or seasonally. With this procedure you can see at a glance which children are absent, and youngsters will soon recognize their names and their classmates' names.

T. M. Hanak—Preschool, Linden Little Rascals, Linden, MI

Attendance

Smiling Faces

To make taking attendance a simple matter and help young-sters practice name recognition, create this management display using pictures of students' smiling faces. Request that a home-supplies store donate countertop samples that are no longer in use. Trim a child's photo; then mount it onto a sample and label the back of the sample with the child's name. Screw a class supply of cup hooks into a piece of wood so that they are evenly spaced and in rows. At the beginning of the year, hang the samples on the hooks to reveal the sides showing the children's faces. As each child arrives at school, have him locate his picture and turn his name over. Later in the year, request that each child locate his name and turn his picture over. This quick method will tell you at a glance which children are not present.

Lynn Coleman—Preschool, Tumbling Tykes Preschool, Endwell, NY

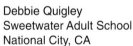

Hang It Out to Try

Little ones will be quick to recognize their names when you hang this attendance-taking method out for a try. From colorful paper, cut a class supply of T-shirt shapes; then label each shape with a different child's name. Store the shirts in a miniature laundry basket along with miniature plastic clothespins. Secure a length of yarn onto a display board at students' level. As each child arrives at school, request that she find the shirt labeled with her name and clip it to the clothesline. Take a look at your display to see who's hanging out with you each day.

Debbie Quigley
Sweetwater Adult School
National City, CA

Taking Attendance

To make taking roll a simple task, make an attendance display. To make this display, mount each child's photo on a construction paper rectangle and label the back with the child's name. Laminate. Punch a hole at the top of each rectangle and attach a length of string. Attach the string to a bulletin board. Turn each rectangle to reveal the side show-ing the child's name. As each child arrives at school, have him locate his name and turn his picture over. Names still showing on the bulletin board will indicate at a glance who's not present.

Debbie Miller—Pre/K, Rockingham County Headstart, Eden, NC

Reach for the Stars

Here's a classroom display idea that will have your children reaching for the stars to assist you with the attendance. Personalize an instant photo of each child and adult worker in your classroom. For each child and worker, cut a construction paper star shape that is large enough to frame a photo. Next, cut a house shape from a 12" x 18" piece of construction paper. If desired, laminate the stars and house shape for durability. Attach the hook side of a piece of self-adhesive Velcro fastener to the middle of each star. Attach several hook-side pieces of Velcro fastener to the house. Then attach the loop side of a piece of Velcro fastener to the back of each photo. Mount the house at students' level and mount the stars within students' reach. Title your display. Store the photos nearby.

Each day, as a child enters, have her go to the display, locate her photo, and attach it to a star. After everyone enters, ask a designated helper to attach the photos of the absent students and workers to the house. You'll know at a glance who is present for the day. In return, all of your students will gain a sense of responsibility for helping out by reaching for the stars!

Melinda Davidson—Integrated Special Needs Preschool
Brockton Early Childhood Program
Brockton, MA

Who's at the Zoo Today?

You'll save precious moments using this teacher-free attendance-taking method, and your students will practice name recognition and responsibility at the same time. Make a zoo picture similar to the one shown. For each child in your class, glue a personalized library pocket onto the picture. Laminate the resulting chart for durability. Use a craft blade to cut open each child's library pocket. Then display the chart for child accessibility. Personalize a rectangular slip of paper for each child to resemble a zoo ticket. On the first day of school have each child match his name on his ticket to the correct pocket. Just a glance will let you know who's at school today.

As each child leaves for the day, have him remove his ticket and deposit it in a container. The next morning, each child gets more name-recognition practice as he sorts through the tickets to find his name. In no time at all, youngsters catch on to the routine and roll call can be taken with just a glance.

Attendance

A Warm and Woolly Welcome

Let little lambs welcome your little ones to school each day! Begin by using craft paints to create a meadow scene on a large, rectangular cookie sheet. Hot-glue eyelet lace trim around the edges of the pan. Hang the cookie-sheet meadow on your classroom wall. From construction paper, cut one large lamb shape and a classroom supply of smaller lamb shapes. Laminate the cutouts. Write on the large cutout "Who's Here Today?" Mount the larger lamb above the cookie sheet. Label each smaller lamb with a different child's name. Attach a piece of magnetic tape to the back of each lamb. Place the lambs on a table or store them in a container. As each child enters the classroom, have her find her lamb and place it in the cookie-sheet meadow to let you—the mother lamb—know she is present.

Martha A. Briggs
Rosemont Tuesday/Thursday School
Fort Worth, TX

"I Am Here!"

Take attendance and help little ones practice name recognition with this management aid. Personalize a decorated index card or seasonal cutout for each child. Cut one piece of Velcro tape for each cutout. Peel the paper off the back of each Velcro piece. Attach the loop side of each piece to the back of a different card or cutout. On a wall, within your youngsters' reach, mount the hook side of each Velcro tape piece. Attach the cards or cutouts to the wall. Make a large tagboard pocket and program the front of it with "I am here." Then mount the pocket on the wall. Each morning, as each student enters your room, have him locate his nametag, remove it from the wall, and place it in the "I am here" pocket. With this quick and easy method, you can tell at a glance which children are present.

Debbie Brown—Four-Year-Olds
Corson Park Day Care
Millville, NJ

This Must Be the Place

Your preschoolers will know right where to go when they see this lineup of colorful T-shirts outside your door. To make the display, cut out two narrow lengths of bulletin board paper and tape them to your wall to resemble clothesline poles. Next, attach the ends of a length of thick yarn to the poles to serve as the clothesline. Cut out eight large T-shirt shapes from different colors of construction paper. Use a wide-tipped marker to label each of the seven shirts with a different letter from the word "Welcome." Then label the eighth shirt with your name and room number. Mount each shirt to the wall so that it slightly overlaps the clothesline. Finish the display by clipping colorful clothespins to the shoulders of each shirt as shown. Glad you're here!

The Magic Apples of My Eye

Let each child know how important he is to you with this "magic" idea that plants a seed of wonder. In advance, cut out a large tagboard apple for each child in your class. Using a craft blade, cut out a square from the center of each apple. (Judge the size of the apple and the cutout square by the size of your Polaroid pictures—described later.) If desired, add a stem and leaf to each apple. Then mount a large tree cutout on a classroom wall. On the first day of school, take each child's picture with a Polaroid camera. Invite each child to hold his picture by the edges and watch as the "magic" happens! When each photo has developed, glue it to the back of an apple and write the child's name on the front of the apple. Mount each apple on the tree and title the display "The Apples of [your name]'s Eye!" After explaining the meaning of the title to your students, watch them shine with pride!

Lou Monger, Glen Allen Elementary, Glen Allen, VA

Here Are My Hands

Dip your hands into this first-day memento that will mean a lot to both children and parents. To begin, copy the poem below on white paper; then duplicate it for each child. Next have each child select a color of paint and make handprints on the top part of a sheet of construction paper. When the paint is dry, glue the poem to the bottom part. Read the poem together, inviting each child to read along. Also encourage each child to count the ten fingers in her handprints and on her own hands. That sounds like a very good day!

Here are my hands with ten fingers in all—
My first mark in school to hang on the wall.
As years go by, I'll remember and say,
"My hands and I had a very good day!"

Melissa Jackson, Miano School, Los Banos, CA

Trendy Tees

Use this idea to practice fine-motor skills and encourage creativity with your little fashion designers. Make several simple T-shirt templates from tagboard. Have each child choose a color of construction paper; then help her trace and cut out a shirt shape. Use a marker to label each child's shirt with her name. Then provide a variety of decorative materials—such as glitter glue, stickers, and fabric scraps—for each child to use to decorate her T-shirt. When the projects are complete, remove the T-shirts that spell "Welcome" on the clothesline created in "This Must Be the Place" (page 9). Then hang the new T-shirt collection on the clothesline. (You might need to add another clothesline to accommodate everyone's shirt.) Finish the display by adding the title "Look Who's Hanging Out in Our Room!" These one-of-a-kind T-shirts are sure to be conversation starters for anyone hangin' around in the hallway.

LOOK WHO'S HANGING OUT IN OUR ROOM!

Katie   Cassie   Jamar   Noah   Deanna   Allen

Oh, You'll Know!

Every parent who has dealt with the question, "How will I know who my teacher is?" will be forever grateful to you for this idea! Choose a symbol from a classroom theme or a book that you plan to read on the first day. Then design something with that symbol that you can wear. For example, if you plan to read *The Cat in the Hat,* make a red-and-white striped hat from a paper plate and construction paper. (See additional suggestions below.) A couple of weeks before school starts, jot a quick note to each child telling her that you will be the teacher wearing (for example) the tall, red-and-white striped hat. They'll know just what to look for!

- For a teddy bear theme, wear a headband with teddy bear ears.
- For a T-shirt theme, wear a very colorful, oversized T-shirt.

Deb Scala
Mt. Tabor Elementary School
Mt. Tabor, NJ

First Week Theme

Help youngsters locate their classroom easily with a special color-coordinated theme for the first week of school. Meet with your kindergarten colleagues to determine a different color and related theme for each class. Prior to the first day of school, give or mail each parent a personalized shape nametag for his youngster to wear on the first day. Attach a trail of corresponding shapes onto the floor leading to your classroom door. On your door, mount a large character shape programmed to welcome your youngsters. The color-coded path and character make it easy for youngsters to find their classroom.

Cheryl Wellman
Quincy Head Start
Quincy, IL

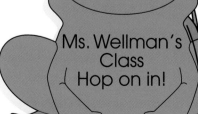

Troy
Amy
Lynn

Ms. Wellman's Class
Hop on in!

Welcome Aboard

Load this bus with each child's self-portrait, and you'll have an attractive room display that each child will feel proud to have a hand in creating. Provide an assortment of skin-toned construction paper and other art supplies such as crayons, yarn, fabric scraps, scissors, and glue. Have each child choose a color of paper and cut out a large circle to represent his head. Then have each child glue his head cut-out onto a white sheet of construction paper and use the art supplies to create a self-portrait. Next, cut out a large yellow school-bus shape from bulletin board paper. Mount the bus cutout and a title on a bulletin board. When each child's self-portrait is complete, assist him in selecting a place on the bus to staple his picture to resemble a child looking out of the bus's window.

Hugs and Kisses

No matter how old you are, making it through the first day of school deserves a hug and a kiss! In advance, purchase a supply of Hershey's Hugs and Kisses candies. For each child, wrap a Hug and a Kiss together in a square of tissue paper; then tie the tissue paper closed with a length of curling ribbon. At the end of the first day, tell your youngsters that they each deserve a hug and a kiss—and then hand them out!

Sandra Rice, Trinity Lutheran School, West Seneca, NY

Parent and Child Pictures

At the beginning of the year, do you find it challenging to learn your students' names and match the students with their parents? This idea will make it a snap! When each parent and child arrive on the first day of school, put a nametag on the child; then quickly snap a picture of the child with his parent. After school, have the pictures developed at a one-hour photo lab. Study the pictures that night. The next day you'll be able to call each child by name and when dismissal time arrives, recognizing parents will be quick and easy!

Fran Tortorici—Three-Year-Olds
Castleton Hill Moravian Preschool
Staten Island, NY

Back-to-School

Duck, Duck, Who?

That old favorite game of Duck, Duck, Goose is a great one to use when it comes to learning names! First play the game in the traditional way. Then add little twists. For example, when It sits down, ask him to say the name of his chaser. At another time, announce that It must say the goose's name as he chooses her. Or even write each child's name on a goose cutout. Place all the cutouts in a box. Then have It secretly choose a goose from the box. Have him whisper the name to you (for confirmation) and then choose that person as the goose during his turn. You'd better run!

Kelly J. Sickle, Oak Grove Primary, Oak Grove, MD

Mingling Manager

On that first day of school, do you have every intention to meet and greet each new child and parent with warmth and security only to be barraged by too many things happening at once? Here's a suggestion to ease that dilemma. Before students arrive, set up several play dough stations on your tables. If desired, offer written suggestions at each station to get the dough rolling—so to speak! When children and parents arrive, ask them to choose a place to work with the play dough. Because each parent and child is involved in this activity, you'll be able to meet and mingle at your leisure. You're also likely to find that this environment is a great one in which students and parents get to know each other as well. So let's get that dough rolling!

Leslye Davidson, Alameda, CA

We're So Glad You're in Our Classroom!

Use this little song as you bring closure to the end of your first school day. Singing it together will help students remember each other's names, and help each child feel welcome and special. Make a classroom quantity of the award pattern (page 71) on construction paper. Personalize and sign an award for each child. Then seat your youngsters in a circle. Sing the song below, inserting your school's name and several of your students' names each time you repeat it until you have mentioned each child in your classroom. As you sing each child's name, give her personalized award to her. Then sing the last verse, inserting the appropriate day of the week.

(sung to the tune of "The More We Get Together")

We're so glad you're in our classroom, our classroom, our classroom.
We're so glad you're in our classroom at [school's name].
We're glad to have [David], and [Amy], and [Jessica].
We're so glad you're in our classroom at [school's name].

We'll see you all on [Tuesday], on [Tuesday], on [Tuesday].
We'll see you all on [Tuesday], at [school's name].

Tradition! Tradition!

Cakes, candles, ice cream, or pie; presents, cards, games, or rides—any way you slice it, a birthday is fun! Prompt your youngsters to think of the ways that their families celebrate birthdays. Ask them to share their birthday traditions with the group. As youngsters share, write their responses on a large gift-shaped cutout. Afterward share and discuss the birthday history and birthday traditions listed below.

- A long, long time ago, it was thought that only kings or very important men were special enough to celebrate their birthdays. What do your students think of that?

- The Germans were the first people to use lighted candles on birthday cakes. They thought that the birthday person's secret wish might be granted if the candles were all blown out with one puff! Find out if any of your students' birthday wishes have come true.

- Playing games at birthday parties started a long time ago. They were usually games of skill or strength intended to show how much progress a child had made over the last year. What games do your students like to play at their own parties?

Birthday Traditions

- My family always gets pizza every time!
  Tasha

- We go to my grandma's house and she makes a cake with balloons on it.
  Ben

- At my house the birthday person eats dinner off a special red plate.
  Jackson

Second Verse

Add a little action and some counting fun to the singing of "Happy Birthday to You!" When you sing the song to a child, have your youngsters add this second verse.

We'll clap for your years.
We'll clap for your years.
We'll clap and give cheers.
We'll clap for your years.
One, two, three, four, five, six— *Clap one time for each year of the child's age as you count aloud.*

Yea, [Child's name]!

Birthday Bookbag

A chosen literature selection just might be the icing on the cake for your special birthday boy or girl. Fill a festive birthday gift bag with your favorite birthday books. In the morning, encourage the birthday child to look through the books. At storytime, present the bag to that child and have her select a book to be read aloud in her honor.

Birthdays

Creative Collages

Take a breath and make a birthday wish for the creation of creative collages. Stock an art center with geometric shapes cut from birthday-style wrapping paper. Also provide birthday-related construction paper die-cuts, curling ribbon, birthday-related stickers, used birthday cards, large sheets of colorful construction paper, scissors, and glue. As students visit the art center, encourage them to use their choice of the provided materials to make a collage. Top each collage with a bow and personalized gift tag; then display it near the center.

Birthday Royalty

Everyone celebrating a birthday deserves to feel like a king or queen. Set up a birthday crown–making station at your art center for your birthday royalty. Cut crown shapes from wrapping paper or construction paper; then mount the shapes onto colorful sentence strips. Provide a variety of art supplies such as wrapping paper scraps, metallic paper, glitter, colored glue, and scissors for decorating the crowns. Happy birthday, Your Majesty!

Birthday Gems

Create a brilliant display to put a little sparkle into each child's birthday. Make 12 white construction paper gemstones similar to the ones shown. Use watercolor paints to paint each one to resemble a different month's birthstone. Glue each gemstone to a construction paper ring; then laminate the rings. Program the band of each ring with the name of the gemstone and the corresponding month of the year. Write each child's name on the appropriate birthstone. Mount all of the rings and a title on a bulletin board. Place a supply of toy rings in a resealable bag and pin the bag to a corner of the board. On each child's birthday, give him an opportunity to choose a ring from the bag. What may only cost you a dime might make each little birthday person feel like a million bucks!

Karen G. Barrow, Ethel Jacobsen, Surf City, NJ

Play Dough Party Place

Join the fun at the play dough party place where birthday cakes are the focus of the fun. Collect disposable tart pans, potpie tins, and muffin pans. Place the pans in a center along with play dough, birthday candles or cut straws, craft sticks or plastic knives, and festive paper plates. Let's make a cake!

Everyone's Included!

If you have children whose birthdays occur during the summer and your school is not in session, celebrate half-birthdays for those children. Help each child count six months from his birthday month, and declare that month and his actual birth date to be his half-birthday. Celebrate the half-birthdays with all the regular birthday trimmings.

Tara Stefanich, Merritt Elementary School, Mt. Iron, MN

A Birthday Bundle

A take-home bundle is a bona fide way to thrill every birthday boy or girl. Fill a backpack, bookbag, large birthday gift bag, or decorated, handled plastic box with a collection of birthday goodies. Consider including some of these items:

- a birthday-related picture book
- a videocassette of a birthday-related story
- a stuffed toy dressed in a vest or bandana made from festive fabric
- a recipe for a special birthday treat such as cookies or cupcakes
- birthday party supplies such as noisemakers, birthday hats, and festive plates
- a goodie bag of inexpensive prizes
- crayons and a class birthday book (Bind blank paper between laminated wrapping paper covers.)
- a note to caregivers requesting that they assist the child in drawing a picture in the birthday book and record the child's dictated description of his special day

Request that the bundle of materials (excluding the goodie bag and party supplies) be returned after one week.

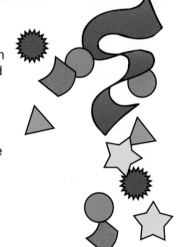

It's a Party, and Everyone's Invited!

Turn your dramatic-play area into party central. Purchase or have the children help you decorate a birthday banner. Suspend the banner over the area along with colorful streamers. Stock the center with birthday plates, cups, napkins, paper and crayons, gift-wrapped boxes, and hats.

To make a permanent birthday cake for the center, spread plaster of paris over the top and sides of a cake-shaped piece of polystyrene foam. Before the plaster sets, insert birthday candles or candleholders. Add decorative details to the cake with plaster that has been tinted with food coloring, or decorate the top of the cake with colored glue once the plaster is dry. If desired, hot-glue fabric trims to the base of the cake.

As children visit the center, seize the opportunity to reinforce math skills and language development as youngsters prepare invitations, set the birthday table, and more. What a celebration station!

Birthday Bulletin Board

Spotlight your current birthday boy or girl with a bulletin board that has presence. Mount wrapping paper on a bulletin board; then add the title "Happy Birthday to You!" In advance of each child's birthday, send a note home requesting pictures of the child and other mountable items related to the child's interests. If possible, feature each child during the week before or after her birthday. Assign a special week for students who have birthdays during the summer or school holidays. Be sure to provide time for the birthday boy or girl to discuss with the class the pictures and items chosen for display. Don't forget to include yourself during your own special week or feature yourself during open house to introduce yourself to parents!

Birthday Reports

Now that you've established that everyone has a birthday, it's time to get down to the specifics. Make a birthday report form similar to the one shown. Then make a copy for each child. Invite each child to color her page; then have her take it home to be completed with the help of a parent or other adult. Encourage each child to bring her completed report back to school, along with a baby picture of herself. *(Tell students to bring their baby pictures straight to you and not to show them to anyone else!)* When all the reports and pictures are in, display the baby pictures (unnamed) on a bulletin board or wall, leaving spaces to mount reports between pictures. Secretly add a baby picture of yourself to the collection. During a group time, have each child share her report with the class. After each report is shared, encourage the rest of the class to guess which picture belongs to the report giver. When the picture is correctly identified, mount the report next to that picture. Are there any surprises? When children figure out that the last picture is you, share your own completed birthday report with your class.

All-in-One Calendar

With these all-in-one calendar pieces, you can help children learn calendar skills, weather, numeral recognition, counting, and even graphing! For each type of weather—sunny, cloudy, rainy, and snowy—prepare a set of 31 numbered calendar markers as shown. During your daily calendar time, record the date using the marker with the appropriate numeral and weather symbol. At the end of each month, regroup the daily markers by the weather symbol to create a graph. How many days were rainy this month? Three! Days 3, 27, and 30!

Patricia Parahus—PreK
Our Redeemer
Levittown, NY

Stick 'em Up!

Tired of rolling tape in order to adhere calendar markers to your calendar? Try this sticky tip! Laminate your calendar, daily markers, and an extra sheet of poster board. Squeeze a drop of Aleene's Tack-It Over & Over glue onto the back of each marker. Allow the glue to dry. Stick the markers on the extra sheet of poster board to store them. During your calendar time, stick the day's marker on your calendar. These pieces will stick to your calendar over and over again!

Judy Kuhn Skaggs—Three-Year-Olds, Highland Preschool, Raleigh, NC

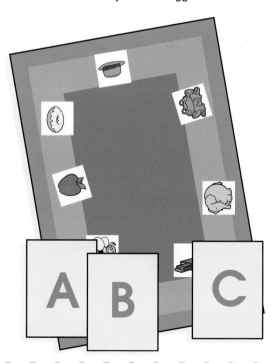

ABC Tickets

Try this novel idea for seating your youngsters during circle time. In advance, tape alphabet picture cards in a circle on the rug. Every morning as each student arrives, provide him with a letter card or "ticket" that corresponds with a picture card. Have each child locate his spot on the rug by matching the letter and picture cards. For a variation, have youngsters match either uppercase and lowercase letters or number words and numerals.

Jan McManus
Our Mother of Sorrows
Cincinnati, OH

Calendar and Circle Time

Mary Wore Her Red Dress

Feature each child's name and chosen specialty of the day with this familiar song. First, share the book *Mary Wore Her Red Dress and Henry Wore His Green Sneakers,* adapted and illustrated by Merle Peek. Then have each child stand, in turn, and say her name and what she would like the class to sing about. Then sing away! Extend the use of this song by using it in call-and-response style to encourage children to remember their classmate's names. To do so, sing the song asking a question, such as "Who is wearing stripes today?" or "Who is wearing brown boots?" Encourage the class to respond by singing, for example, "Jess is wearing stripes today, stripes today, stripes today…"

Judy Richmond
Good Shepherd Lutheran
Pekin, IL

This Is What I Can Do

If your youngsters are full of the wiggles at circle time, then this activity might just be the ticket! Say the verse below. After the last line, indicate a child to be the leader for the next verse and to select the movement for this round. Continue in this manner until each child has had a turn to be the leader.

This is what I can do.	*Demonstrate action such as patting your head.*
Everybody do it too!	*Encourage everyone to join in.*
This is what I can do.	*Continue movement.*
Now I'll pass it on to you!	*Point to someone who then leads the next verse.*

Jean Lindquist, Zion Lutheran School, Cologne, MN

Dressed for the Weather

These easy-to-make weather folks will be a great addition to your daily circle-time weather discussions. Cut simple people shapes from cork (available in rolls from craft stores and home supply superstores). Also cut simple clothing shapes from a variety of fabrics to represent clothing for different seasons. Attach the cork shapes to a wall or display. During your group time, ask children to help you select clothing that is appropriate for the day's weather. Then use pushpins to attach the clothes to the cork people shapes.

Amy Aloi
Prince Georges County Head Start
Berkshire Elementary
Forestville, MD

Classroom Jobs and Helpers

A Special Teddy Bear

Here's a warm and fuzzy way to display your helper's name each day. For each child, personalize a construction paper heart cutout and punch a hole in each cutout. Every morning, select one child to be the helper of the day. Then thread the corresponding cutout onto a length of yarn. Tie the yarn around a teddy bear's neck and display this fuzzy friend on your desk. Your little ones will be anxious to see who the helper is each day.

Laurie Matt—Preschool
Christ the King School
Overland Park, KS

Money

Your students are sure to cash in with this idea that's rich on classroom responsibilities. Make a chart with each student's name on it. Assign each student a job or responsibility to be done by the end of the day. Before dismissal, check to see that each student's job has been completed. If so, place a check on the chart next to his name. Each check is worth five cents of play money. Each Friday is payday when the checks are added up and the children are paid. The plastic coins are placed in a student-made bank (such as a converted juice can) until Monday. On Monday the students are permitted to use their earnings in a classroom store made up of various inexpensive items. This money idea sure makes "cents"!

Maria Gray, S. S. Conner Elementary, Dallas, TX

Two by Two

When a task seems a bit overwhelming, teamwork is the ticket to get the job done! Assign selected classroom jobs to teams of two. For example, you might choose two people to accomplish a larger task such as cleaning up your block area. Ask the team members to work together to devise a plan to get the job done. Encourage them to support each other by complimenting one another's good work. Big jobs don't seem quite as big when you approach them two by two!

Julie Maffett
Child Care Association
Cocoa, FL

Classroom Jobs and Helpers

Anybody Know a Good Photographer?

Sure, a whole lot of 'em! Instead of taking time out to be your own photographer, assign the job to your students. At the beginning of the year, use an old camera to teach children how to take photographs. Keep the camera in your dramatic-play area for practice. When you think students have the hang of it, create a press badge and a paper bag vest. Then, at each different event, assign a different child to wear the badge and vest and be the class photographer with a real disposable camera. Tell each child how many pictures she can take and then leave the rest up to artistic interpretation!

Ericka Way
Leslie Fox Keyser Elementary
Front Royal, VA

Playground Pals

Gathering up your playground equipment is made simple when you have Playground Pals. In advance, label a sheet of paper with the names of your playground toys and a simple drawing of each one (as shown). Laminate the page; then put it on a clipboard. When you're ready to go to the playground, have your chosen Playground Pal use a dry-erase marker to check off each item that is going out. When you come back inside, have that helper check each item in. If anything is missing, your Playground Pal can alert you right away and lead the search.

adapted from an idea by AnnaLisa R. Damminger

Blooming Leaders

Flowers can signal more than the arrival of spring when you use this idea! They can also signal a student that it's her turn to be the class leader. Cut a flower for each child from colorful construction paper. Add a yellow circle center personalized with a child's name to each flower. Then glue each child's flower to a separate craft stick stem. On each child's turn to be the leader, place her flower in a small flowerpot. Use a lump of green clay to hold the flower upright; then fill the pot with green Easter grass.

Lynne Greene—Four-Year-Olds
First Baptist Church Preschool
Greensboro, NC

Classroom Jobs and Helpers

Zoo Staff

Your kids will take pride in their official titles when it's their turn to be on the zoo staff—and classroom maintenance will go on without a hitch! Post the titles and corresponding job descriptions on your helpers bulletin board. Discuss the importance and responsibilities of each job with your youngsters. Then pin on nametags to indicate who is responsible for which job. Rotate names or add other children's names as often as you like.

Staff Meetings

How important your little ones will feel when they get to attend staff meetings! If you assign classroom jobs by the week, hold a staff meeting midway through the week. After discussing areas of concern and praise, send your little workers off to complete their term of service with pride!

Vivi Sadel, Finletter School, Philadelphia, PA

Who's Helping?

Need an easy-to-change classroom helpers chart? Use a behind-the-door shoe organizer that has clear pockets. For each pocket, label a piece of tagboard with a different classroom job. Place a tagboard label in each pocket. Then place a different child's photo or nametag in each pocket to designate your daily or weekly helpers. When it's time for new helpers, simply rearrange or replace the pictures or nametags in the pockets.

Kimberly Filip, Oakman Preschool, Dearborn, MI

Classroom Jobs and Helpers

Helpers in Bloom

Plant a bouquet of helpers with this seasonal management idea. Cut out a flower shape for each student in your class. Attach a small photo of each child to the center of her flower as a special touch. Mount each flower on a large craft stick; then label each flower with the appropriate student's name. Decoratively paint a flowerpot; then fill the pot with rice or sand. Stand the flower sticks in the pot. When you need a helper, delicately pick a flower from the pot. Once every child has had an opportunity to help, replant your flowers so they can bloom again.

Karen Keenan—4-year-olds
Little Friends Preschool
Yorba Linda, CA

Table Toppers

If it's on a table, Table Toppers come to the rescue! Each week, assign a team of children to be Table Toppers. Then, when anything pops up that involves a table, you know just where your help is. Table Toppers can set the table, clean messy tables, pass out supplies, etc. If it's on a table, they're tops!

AnnaLisa R. Damminger, Mullica Hill, NJ

Derrick
Supplies Clerk

Teacher's Helpers

Before an anticipated absence, assign jobs to youngsters who are capable of being good assistants and for whom the responsibility of such a task would be motivating. Designate a rules official who can answer the substitute teacher's questions about general classroom regulations. Select a supplies clerk to assist the substitute in finding the materials needed. Also designate an attendance helper and a hall monitor. Explain each child's responsibility to him and place a note of explanation and helper necklace tag with the substitute's materials.

Michelle Sears
Corinth Headstart
Glens Falls, NY

Cleanup Matchup

Here's a transition tip that aids in color recognition, speeds up cleanup time, and promotes cooperation among youngsters. Mount a large paper circle on the wall in each area of your room, using a different color for each area. Cut and laminate a set of smaller circles of each color so that the total number of circles equals the number of children in your class. When it's cleanup time, ask each child to select a laminated circle and clean the area of the room that displays the same color of circle. As a variation for older children, provide cards labeled with color words. Or label the centers with numerals and provide cards labeled with dot sets.

Barbara Wagner—Preschool
Higgelty Piggelty Preschool
Allison, IA

Cleanup Call

Keep your students focused on the task of cleaning up with this cute call-and-response song. Signal cleanup time by singing the first line of the song. Continue singing until the room is clean and you're ready for your next activity.

Clean Up
(sung to the tune of "The Banana Boat Song")

Teacher:	Clean up!
Students:	Clee-ee-ee-ee-ean up!
Teacher:	Clean up your space and check out the floor!
Students:	Clean up our space and check out the floor!
	Clean up our space and check out the floor!

Deb Scala, Mt. Tabor Elementary, Mt. Tabor, NJ

Cleanup Containers

Motivate your preschoolers to pitch in at cleanup time with this nifty idea! Purchase a class supply of medium-size plastic baskets, and then place a few in each area of your classroom. At cleanup time, encourage each child to fill his basket with items that need to be picked up, such as manipulatives, blocks, and so forth. When the basket is full, have the child transfer the contents of his basket to the appropriate storage area. Everybody do your part!

Kathryn Logan—Special Education Preschool
Alaiedon Elementary School
Mason, MI

Scrap Happy!

You're sure to have some scrap-happy helpers when you try this easy cleanup tip! Use masking tape to attach a paper bag to each worktable. Then, during small-group times, encourage children to place their paper scraps in the bags. When the bags are full, just recycle—bags, scraps, and all!

Andrea Henderson—PreK
Jefferson Brethren Preschool
Goshen, IN

The Cleanup Express

Get on the right track and make your room spotless as your youngsters climb aboard the Cleanup Express. Each day when it's cleanup time, blow a train whistle. Then say, "All aboard the Cleanup Express," and invite youngsters to line up behind you. "Chug" around the room, making stops at each area or center, and have your little ones tidy up. What a fun way to get the job done! Toot, toot, puff, puff!

Ann Gudowski—PreK and K

A Tidy Tip

Here's a neat tip that works wonders when youngsters do cut-and-paste activities. Place several damp cloths in each of several plastic margarine containers. Place a container and an empty coffee can on each table. After a cut-and-paste activity, have youngsters place their scrap papers in the cans and then wipe their hands with the wet cloths for easy cleanup.

Adapted from an idea by Jo-Ellen Forrest
St. Louis Public Schools
St. Louis, MO

9 Ways to Clean Our Room

1. Clean up the floor.
2. Empty the trash.
3. Wipe off the tables.
4. Straighten the papers.
5. Push in the chairs.
6. Erase the board.
7. Put the crayons away.
8. Straighten the cubbies.
9. Wipe out the sink.

Counting on Help

Here's an idea for those days when the cleanup is a little too much for individual classroom helpers. Start by choosing a number, such as nine. Then ask the class to brainstorm nine ways to clean up the room. Write their responses on a chart. Have a different small group of children volunteer for each different idea listed. Then divide and conquer!

Michele Griffith, Duffy Elementary, West Hartford, CT

Scrub-a-dub-dub

Use these easy tips to clean small plastic manipulatives. Load the manipulatives inside mesh laundry bags (such as those used for delicate items), place them inside a washing machine with detergent and bleach, and run the machine on a normal cycle. Or place the bag of items in the dishwasher. (Do not use the dry cycle.) Squeaky clean manipulatives!

Lauren Sommerer—Preschool, St. John Child Development Center, Seward, NE

Happy Helpers

You'll have lots of happy helpers when you employ this cleanup time-management tip! From laminated yellow construction paper, prepare a class supply of smiley faces. Write each child's name on a separate face. To signal that it's time to clean up, hand each child his smiley face. When he has completed his cleaning tasks, have him return it to you. Then use Sticky-Tac adhesive to attach the face to a display titled "Happy Helpers." When your room is clean, everyone will be all smiles!

adapted from an idea by Anita Edlund—Three-Year-Olds
Cokesbury Children's Center, Farragut, TN

Libby

Cleanup

Staple Remover

Do you end up with staples on your floor or carpet when you change your bulletin boards? Try this cleanup tip! After removing staples from a display, have a student take a horseshoe magnet and run it along the floor beneath the bulletin board to catch those wayward staples. Your preschoolers will love this "attractive" cleanup job!

Althea A. Bleckley
South Rabun Elementary
Tiger, GA

Three Minutes

During the last few minutes of each day, enlist the help of your students with this timely cleanup tip. Choose a cleanup helper to set and monitor a timer for three minutes. Challenge your youngsters to quietly clean up before the sand slips through the timer or the bell on the timer rings. Have your cleanup helper alert your students when time is about to expire. With this quick and easy method, your room will be spotless in a matter of minutes.

Pat Bollinger, Leopold R–3, Leopold, MO

Litter Jugs

If you want a solution for messy tables, then try this neat tip. Cut off the top portion of a one-gallon milk jug (keeping the handle intact). Place one milk jug on each table. Throughout the day, have youngsters discard paper scraps and trash in the jug. At the end of each day, designate one child from each table to empty the jug. This is a sure way to keep cleanup simple and your room spotless.

Sharon Walker
Danville Elementary
Danville, AL

Molly Mop

Use a charismatic character named Molly Mop to announce cleanup time in your classroom. To make Molly, cut off a few pieces from one side of a colorful foam dish mop. To that side of the mop, hot-glue half of a polystyrene ball. Put on two wiggle eye stickers and a red felt mouth to complete Molly's face. Then cut out a dress shape from tagboard and glue it to the mop's handle. As a signal, ask a special helper to hold up Molly Mop. What time is it, Molly Mop? It's cleanup time!

Martha Whitaker—Three- and Four-Year-Olds
Loving Start Preschool, Whitefish Bay, WI

Cleanup Freeze

Turn cleanup time into fun time! Play a song as children clean up from an activity or from playtime. Throughout the song, stop the music and have everyone freeze. Restart the music to get little ones moving again. Cleanup will be a breeze when you play the freeze!

Debbie Brown—Four- and Five-Year-Olds
Corson Park Day Care
Millville, NJ

BLOCKS

Cleanup

Responsibility Chart

To guarantee that everyone participates during cleanup time, use a responsibility chart. Cut out catalog pictures of the various types of toys, games, and manipulatives that are used in your classroom. Glue these pictures to a sheet or two of tagboard, and label each picture. Laminate the chart. Post each child's picture next to the job for which he will be responsible. At cleanup time, your happy helpers need only to glance at the chart to see which areas they are to clean up. Periodically change job responsibilities by moving the self-sticking notes.

Coreen VanDerWoude
Rochester Christian School
Rochester, NY

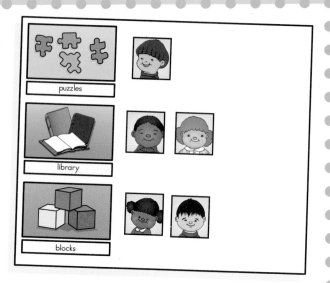

Cleanup Song

Your room will sparkle at cleanup time when you use a decorated wand called Mr. Twinkle. Glue a tagboard star cutout to the end of a 12-inch wooden dowel. Then when it's time to clean up, lightly tap each youngster on the shoulder with Mr. Twinkle as you sing this song:

(sung to the tune of "Twinkle, Twinkle, Little Star")

Twinkle, twinkle, little star,
Time to clean up where you are.
Put each toy back in its place.
Keep a smile on your face.
Twinkle, twinkle, little star,
Time to clean up where you are.

Jeanne Taylor—PreK, YMCA Preschool, Thornton, CO

Tickets, Please

Promote a clean classroom with this quick pick up. Just before your youngsters line up to leave the classroom, announce that they will need tickets in order to leave the room. A ticket is a given number of craps of paper (or whatever is necessary to clean the room). Wait by the door with a wastebasket as each child deposits her ticket before leaving. The children love the idea, and the room gets cleaned. Now that's the ticket!

Debbie Palmer—Preschool
A New Beginning Christian School
Cleveland, GA

Cleanup Snakes!

Cleanup will be a "sssnap" when using cleanup snakes. To make a cleanup snake, decorate an old tube sock to resemble a snake. Keep a quantity of these critters in a basket so students will have easy access to them. When it's time to clean up a dirty tabletop, shelf, or floor, have a youngster put a clean-up snake on his hand and slither away to wipe up the mess.

Evelyn Moses
Raleigh Christian Academy
Durham, NC

I Spy

Play a quick game of I Spy to facilitate cleanup time. Announce that you spy a mystery item that needs to be put away; then encourage the cleaning to get under way. When cleanup time is over, announce the mystery item and reward the child who put it away with a sticker. Then give everyone a sticker for working together on a job well done.

Debbie Brown—Four- and Five-Year-Olds, Corson Park School Millville, NJ

Water at Your Fingertips

If you're without a sink in your room and want to eliminate youngsters' unnecessary trips to the restroom sink, then try this helpful hint. In advance, fill a spray bottle with water. Keep it nearby throughout the day and spritz the water to clean up spills, messy fingers, and tables.

Dianne Giggey
Episcopal Day School
Pensacola, FL

Conferences

Coffee and Conversation

Parents will quickly reply after getting these student-painted invitations to parent/teacher conferences or group information sessions. For each child, trace a coffee cup shape (similar to the one shown) onto a large, folded piece of construction paper. Cut out the shape, leaving the fold intact so that the invitation can be opened. Ask a child to paint the front of the invitation using very strong room-temperature coffee. When the coffee is dry, program the inside of each invitation with a message; then send it home. Now get that coffee brewing, and soon you'll be percolating flavorful conversations!

Nancy Goldberg—Three-Year-Olds
B'nai Israel Schilit Nursery School
Rockville, MD

Dear Mom and Dad,

You are invited for coffee and conversation on Monday, November 9, from 9:30–10:30 A.M. Mrs. Goldberg and Mrs. Speisman will be sharing wonderful stories with you! Plus, you can enjoy the yummy lemon snaps that we made. RSVP to my teachers.

Love,
Nancy

Preschoolers Can!

Parents are sure to enjoy looking at this display while waiting for conferences or during an open house. And, as a bonus, it gives a positive message about the many things preschoolers can do. To make the display, take pictures of small groups of children participating in indoor and outdoor activities. Mount each photo to a piece of construction paper; then label the paper "Preschoolers can [action shown]." Arrange the pictures together on a wall or bulletin board. Later, bind the pages together between covers. Title the book "Preschoolers Can!"

Cindy Lawson
Children's EduCare Center
Ft. Wayne, IN

The Art of Being Prepared

With this simple method, you or your substitute will be well-informed. Write important information (enrollment list, seating chart, schedules, procedures, special considerations, emergency exits, and dismissal routines) on colorful index cards. Or use a photocopier to make reductions of these types of information, cut around the reductions, and glue them to index cards. Attach these cards to your desktop using clear Con-Tact covering. Just try to lose those notes in the paper shuffle. It can't be done!

Lori O'Malley
Dingman Delaware Elementary School
Dingmans Ferry, PA

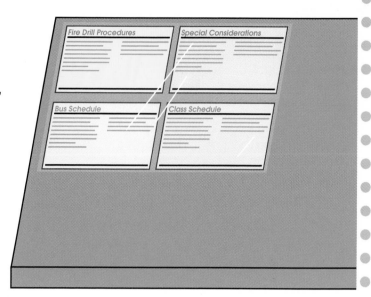

Are We There Yet?

"Is it lunchtime yet?" "When can we go outside?" "Is it time to go home?" Sure, all of these are very important questions to a child—but they also take up a lot of your time, don't they? This idea will help children understand the pace of each day as well as reinforce meaning and print. In advance, laminate a long strip of butcher paper. Glue a school cutout to the left side and a house cutout to the right side. Then use wipe-off markers to program significant times of your day along that strip. Next, add words, simple drawings, and/or pictures to depict your schedule for the first day of school. As you go through the first day, use reusable adhesive to post a cutout (such as a bus or other theme-related item) along the timeline. At the end of the day, program the timeline for the next day. As children become accustomed to this process, ask a child to move the cutout as the day progresses. "I can read just where we are!"

Angela Lavy Joel, Marlowe Elementary, Falling Waters, WV

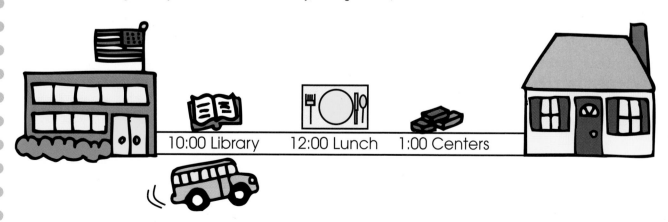

Daily and Weekly Schedules

Rebus Calendar

Use this rebus calendar to help your preschoolers remember on which days they attend special classes or activities. On separate cards or sentence-strip lengths, write each of the days your class attends school and each of your weekly classes and activities, such as art and music. Draw a picture of each of your weekly classes on separate cards, or use photos to represent each activity. To prepare the calendar, display the labels of the days, the pictures of the activities, and the activity labels on a chart or bulletin board as shown. Use an arrow cutout or other symbol to point to the current day. Replace the pictures and labels as needed to include field trips, parties, or other special events.

Mary Jenks—Preschool, Special Education (Hearing Impaired)
Briarlake Elementary
Decatur, GA

Picture Our Day!

This idea provides a great way to reinforce and display your daily schedule. Take photos of students engaged in daily activities from arrival to departure. Next, use clear packing tape to mount three sides of a clear photo sleeve (leaving the sleeve opening intact) for each activity onto a sheet of poster board. Write each activity on a self-adhesive label, attach it to the appropriate photo, and then slide the photo into a sleeve. Display the completed poster near your circle area. During a group time, go over the day's events with students, using time words such as *now, before,* and *after.* Update the photos as seasons and schedules change. You should see what we're doing in preschool today!

Kathy Todd—Three-Year-Olds
Tippecanoe Child Care South
Lafayette, IN

Load 'Em Up, Move 'Em Out

Post a bright bus-shaped cutout on the back of your classroom door, and you have an invaluable dismissal resource. Label the bus with the time that each bus load is to leave. Indicate the names of the students on each load. Similarly post car riders on a car-shaped cutout and walkers on a sneaker-shaped cutout. Also note on the appropriate cutout any special loading procedures that must be followed.

Nancy Dunaway
Hughes Elementary
Forrest City, AR

End-of-the-Day Recap

Gather your little ones around you, and have each of them recall what she did in school today. Start a slap/clap rhythm and encourage your youngsters to join in. Then chant, "Hey, [child's name], what do you say? What did you do in school today?" As the rhythm continues, the child tells something about her day. Continue in this matter until each child has had an opportunity to respond. It's a great way to find out what youngsters consider memorable.

Shelly German
"The Perfect Place" for Children
Pelham, NH

Going Home

Dismissal can be a traumatic time of day for little ones with apprehensions. Help keep them confident and on the right course even when you're away. To accomplish this, keep a recipe holder on your desktop. Label it prominently with a colorful bus cutout so that a substitute can immediately see that it's a resource. Label a card for each child and note his usual transportation. If the youngster is to take an alternate form of transportation, clip the parent's dated permission note to his card. Although this is a great suggestion for keeping a substitute teacher informed, you may find it so helpful on a daily basis that you adapt its use for keeps.

Alvera Bade
Cedar School
Beatrice, NE

Dismissal

Goodbye Song

End your day with this cheerful call-and-response tune that also helps emphasize the order of the days of the week.

Goodbye Song
(sung to the tune of "Are You Sleeping?")

Teacher: Goodbye, children.
Children: Goodbye, teacher.
Teacher: I'll see you soon.
Children: We'll see you soon.
Teacher: See you next on [name of next school day].
Children: See you next on [name of next school day].
Teacher: We'll work and play.
Children: We'll work and play.

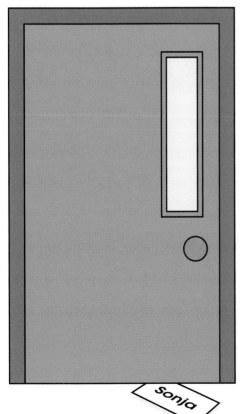

Easy Dismissal

This parent-friendly dismissal routine gives you a chance to say good-bye to each child individually. Write each child's name on a separate index card. Just before dismissal time, place the cards outside your classroom door. When a parent arrives, he slips his child's name card under the door. Quietly help that child gather her things; then deliver her to the parent. Should a parent need to speak to you, suggest that he remain until all of the children have been dismissed.

Joan Banker—Four-Year-Olds
St. Mary's Child Development Center
Garner, NC

Walking Through the Year

The end of the year is the perfect time for this class-made walking book. In advance, collect 11 different-colored sheets of construction paper. Program each of ten of the sheets with a different month of the school year. Title the remaining sheet "Walking Through the Year." For each page, prompt students to recall activities and events that took place during each month, such as field trips, visitors, celebrations, birthdays, and themes. Write the events of each month on that page. Then invite different pairs of students to decorate each page with photos, stickers, and drawings. When the pages are complete, sequence them, beginning with the cover then the September page. Laminate the pages in order and upside down, leaving a small space between each page. (Be sure the pages are aligned and evenly spaced since this book will not be cut apart.) After laminating, trim the side margins and fold the book accordion-style for storage. To read this book, lay it flat and extended on the floor. Invite a child to walk beside each page as he (or the whole class) reads it aloud. You just walked through a whole year!

Barbara Spilman Lawson
Waynesboro, VA

Memory Lane

For the last few weeks of school, invite children, parents, visitors, and other school personnel to stroll down your class's memory lane. To prepare, sort the photos that you've taken throughout the year according to month. Mount each month's pictures on a sheet of labeled poster board. Include child-dictated and teacher captions as desired. Then hang the posters in chronological order in the hall. Near the beginning of this display, mount a poster board street sign labeled "Memory Lane." Everybody loves a trip down memory lane!

June E. Maddox
Calvary Baptist Day School
Savannah, GA

Ice-Cream Sundae Party

Plan this party for the last day of school, and you'll be making sweet memories right up until the last minute! A few days before the end of school, have your students collectively brainstorm ingredients used to make ice-cream sundaes. Assign each of several parent volunteers an ingredient or two to supply for the party. When it's party time, line up the ingredients on a table and assist students in creating the ice-cream sundaes of their dreams.

Ann Scalley—Preschool

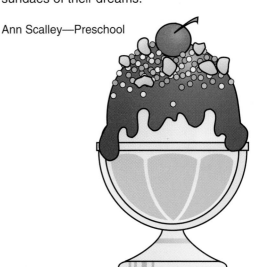

End of the Year

Splash!

Make a splash with this end-of-the-year review game. In advance, prepare a tub of water and some sponges. On blank index cards, write review concepts such as the ones shown. To play the game, choose an outside target. Then divide the class into two to three teams and have them stand in lines. Ask the first child a review question or show him a picture card. If he responds correctly, give him a sponge to throw at the target. If he is incorrect, give the first person on each of the other teams a shot at it. Continue in this manner until all of the cards have been used. Makes ordinary assessment seem kind of dry, doesn't it?

Jaimie K. Hudson, Can-Do Elementary Homeschool Pace, FL

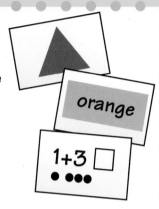

A Memory Book With Visuals

If your end-of-the-year plans include a memory book for each of your students, consider adding two more pages that show how much the youngster has grown during the year. Program the first page of each student's memory book to read "When I started this school year, I was as tall as the string in this pocket." Glue on a paper square to make a pocket. Check your growth chart, and cut a length of yarn equal to the student's first-of-the-year height. Store the string in the pocket. For the second page, cut out a handprint the student made during the beginning of the school year. Glue it to a page programmed to read "My handprint looked like this. See how much I've grown!" When each student's entire memory book is complete, he'll be surprised to see how much he has matured.

Mary Sutula—Preschool, St. Luke's Child Development Center, Orlando, FL

The Very Best Preschoolers

Reminisce over the year's accomplishments with this class-made book that follows the popular pattern in Eric Carle's *The Very Hungry Caterpillar.*

To prepare the book:

1. Caption the first page "One morning the sun came up and—whoosh!—[number of students] little children came to preschool at [school name]. They started to learn."

2. Next, make a page for each month of the school year using this format: "In [month] they [students suggest accomplishments/topics]. But there was still more to learn."

3. For the months of summer vacation, write "During [months], they played and played and played."

4. Caption the last page "Now it was [first month of school] again, and the children were not little preschoolers anymore. They were ready for kindergarten! And there will be lots more to learn!"

After each page is programmed, review *The Very Hungry Caterpillar* with your class. Afterward, share your original text. Then ask student volunteers (or small groups) to illustrate the pages. Bind all the pages together between construction paper covers. After reading the finished book together, encourage your students to share this book with classroom visitors during the last days of school.

Barbara Goldman, Charlotte Sidway School, Grand Island, NY

My Teacher and Me

As the end of the year approaches, do you find those sentimental feelings beginning to creep up on you? Sure, you need and deserve your summer break, but do you feel like you'll actually miss all your little ones (who aren't so little any-more)? Well, this child-made book is a keepsake for you, Teacher! Give each child a sheet of drawing paper and have her illustrate a picture of you and herself. When each child has finished her drawing, encourage her to label the page with your name and hers. Then have her add any other writing or dictation that she'd like. Bind all the pictures between two construction paper covers labeled with the date, grade, and your school. Then ask each child to sign the cover of the book. It's yours to keep, but you just might want to share it with all your students a time or two before they leave!

Maureen Pivnick
North Miami Elementary School
North Miami, FL

Sleeping on a Keepsake

Help each of your children decorate a pillowcase with handprints as a memento of preschool days. Provide a plain, white, prewashed pillowcase for each student, or ask each student to bring one. Using fabric paints, have a child make handprints on his pillow-case and then sign and date it. To permanently set the prints, follow the paint manufacturer's instructions. On the last day of school, send each pillowcase home with its owner.

Candy Blankenship, Lakeside Park Elementary, Hendersonville, TN

A Record Year

Would you like to honor and recognize each of your students for being a member of your class this year? If so, this display makes the top ten list! First, collect old records that you no longer use. Make a hanging loop for each record by threading string through the center hole and then tying the ends into a knot. Hang records at different intervals from the ceiling so that they are arranged around a bulletin board or classroom wall. Then mount several copies of your class picture or each child's individual photo on the board. Also add a few construc-tion paper musical signs and symbols. Title the board "A Record Year With You Here!" Then sit back and bask in the sound effects as the chil-dren see this display—from you to them—for the first time.

Susan Nelson and Dolly Kirchner
John Cline Elementary School
Decorah, IA

Field-Trip Tip

Here's a tip that will keep your youngsters entertained on bus rides. For each child tie a lacing yarn through one of a lacing shape's holes. As each student boards the bus, hand him a shape. Encourage each child to complete his shape, then exchange it with a friend. No more boring bus rides!

Karen Saner
Burns Elementary School
Burns, KS

Seat Belt Matchup

Here's a tip that will help your little ones buckle up quickly and safely when riding in your center's van or bus. Affix matching stickers to the corresponding ends of each seat belt; then cover the stickers with clear tape. Each child can quickly identify his seat belt by simply matching the stickers. Getting safely seated is a snap!

Vail McCole—PreK
Tigger's Treehouse
Grand Junction, CO

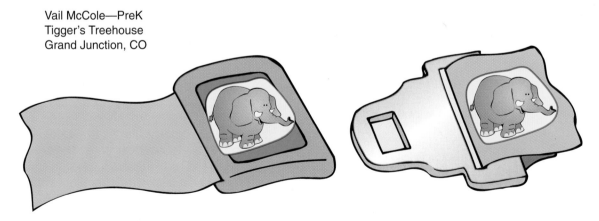

Poultry Party Hats

This festive headgear is sure to get everyone in the mood to party! To make one headband, glue together a 4" x 18" and a 4" x 6" strip of tan construction paper. To the front of the band, glue a five-inch brown circle. Add black paper eyes, a red wattle, and a folded orange square for a beak. Bend several 2" x 18" strips of colorful construction paper in half; then glue the ends to the back of the band for feathers as shown. Finally, fringe the rounded part of two brown half circles; then glue them on the side of the band for wings. Encourage youngsters to put on their hats and strut with pride!

Pumpkin Patch Behavior Tips

Use the theme of the fall season, pumpkins, as a management help. In advance, make a class supply of laminated orange construction paper or tagboard pumpkins. Also make a class supply of large paper pumpkin seeds, write a different child's name on each one, and then put them in a paper bag. When it's time for a group session, invite children over to your pumpkin patch (circle-time area). As each child arrives, put a pumpkin on the floor for him to sit on. If you need for children to take turns during an activity or when you are ready for a transition, simply pull a seed out of your bag and read the name on it.

Henry Fergus, Phoenix, AZ

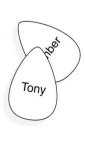

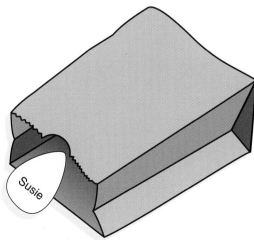

Flower Power

Your classroom management skills will blossom with a little flower power. Cut a set of flower shapes from each of several colors of construction paper. Using clear Con-Tact paper, attach a cutout to each youngster's desk, chair, or work space. When it's time to line up or get materials, call youngsters by groups according to the colors of their flowers. Red flowers may get their coats now.

Kay Tidwell
Savoy ISD
Savoy, TX

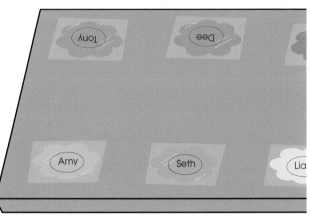

It's Lineup Time

Use this catchy tune to help little ones line up at the end of the day.

(sung to the tune of "Good Night, Ladies")

Goodbye, [student's name].   *Students line up when their names are mentioned.*

Goodbye, [student's name].
Goodbye, [student's name].
It's time to get in line!

Lori Kracoff—Preschool, Lin-wood Community Childcare Center, Lincoln, NH

Step Right Up

You'll be able to invite your line leader to step right up when you use this transition tip. Using a permanent marker, trace a pair of foot shapes onto the center of a carpet square. During group activities or transition times, place the square on the floor to indicate where you would like the line to begin; then request that the line leader for the day step onto the feet. Once your leader's in line, everyone else can find their places. Now that's the way to get those ducks in a row!

Martha Whitaker—Preschool
Loving Start Preschool
Whitefish Bay, WI

Get Your Line In Shape

Little ones will enjoy finding their places in line when you employ this management technique. Make a class supply of several favorite patterns from previous issues of *The Mailbox* onto different colors of paper. Cut out the patterns and label them sequentially with numerals. Arrange the patterns on the floor in a line; then adhere them with clear Con-Tact covering. When it's time to line up, direct a child to find a specified shape, color of shape, or numbered shape. Or allow each child to choose his shape and describe it. Everyone in line? Let's go!

Dawn Hurley—Preschool
Child Care Center
Bethel Park, PA

Zoo Lines

These paw prints will help you eliminate that lineup bunching and crunching. Cut out construction paper paw prints and laminate them. (You might like to consider using different colors of prints to distinguish each set or for patterning purposes.) Position each set of prints where you'd like your students to line up. As children line up, have them place their feet on the paw prints. Just perfect!

Red Line, Green Line

Use colorful tape to create a visual guide that will help your class line up successfully every time! To indicate where your class should stand in line, adhere a strip of yellow tape (long enough for your entire class to stand on) to the floor. Designate the beginning of the lineup area by placing a strip of green tape on the floor so that it is perpendicular to the yellow strip; then similarly designate the end of the area with a red strip. When it's time to line up, ask one child to stand at the beginning of the line on the green strip, have another child stand at the end of the line on the red strip, and then direct the rest of the class to stand on the yellow line that's in between. We're ready to go!

Lisa Marks, Nelson County Elementary Schools, Lovingston, VA

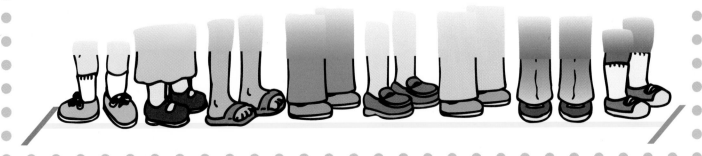

Open House

A Patchwork Quilt of Teachers

Patch together this crafty introduction to your teaching staff for everyone to enjoy during open house. Give each teacher, assistant, support staff, or parent volunteer a sheet of white construction paper. Ask her to fill the sheet with pictures (from photos, magazines, catalogs, postcards, or craft books) that reflect her hobbies, interests, experiences, or talents. Mount each finished sheet on a larger sheet of construction paper of a complementary color. (Alternate background colors if desired.) Then staple the finished projects on a bulletin board, adding additional sections with your favorite quotes on education or warm greetings, if needed. Use a marker to add stitches to give it that quilted look. Everyone will enjoy trying to match each teacher to a quilt section.

Taryn Lynn Way, Los Molinos Elementary School, Los Molinos, CA

Sunshine's Top Ten

This little song booklet will make it easier for parents to sing along with the songs that youngsters have learned in school. You can make a booklet of your students' favorite songs or a few favorites from each of the classes at your level. Type up the favorite songs and collate them into booklets to be given to parents at open house. Then have parents participate in singing several of the songs with their children. Not only is this a lot of fun, but it's also a great icebreaker to have all of the parents singing, dancing, and moving to match the lyrics.

Dena Briscoe, Sunshine Day Care Center, Concord, NC

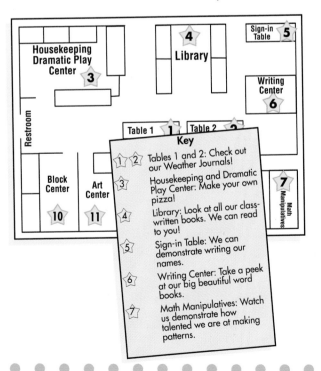

Classroom Walk of Stars

Prepare your little ones to shine during open house with this special guide. In advance, display a numbered star cutout at each point of interest in your classroom. Then draw a simple map of your classroom, using correspondingly numbered stars. Next, write or type a key describing what parents should note at each stop along the way. Then duplicate a supply of the map and key. Before the big night, familiarize your students with the maps so that they'll be able to guide their parents along. As each parent and child arrives for open house, give the parent a map and a key; then encourage the child to guide her parent through all the points of interest on your classroom walk of stars.

Sue Creason
Highland Plaza United Methodist Kindergarten
Hixson, TN

October Open House Reminders

When open house is in October, a colorful way to make sure that students get home with reminders is by using this light-the-jack-o'-lantern idea. Assist each student with making one of the following jack-o'-lantern reminders. To begin, cut a jack-o'-lantern shape from folded construction paper, cut jack-o'-lantern facial features from one side, staple or glue along the left and right edges to form a pocket, and personalize the jack-o'-lantern. Cut out a yellow construction paper copy of a circle bearing the poem message as shown. On the day of open house, show students how their yellow circles can be slipped inside their jack-o'-lantern pockets, "lighting" them. Explain that the jack-o'-lantern pockets will be on their tabletops when parents arrive at open house. Ask each child to show his yellow circle to his parent and to encourage his parent to come to school during open house and light his jack-o'-lantern. When open house is over, you can quickly glance at the jack-o'-lanterns to see who attended and who did not. If you're leaving these projects on the tabletops, light the remaining unlit jack-o'-lanterns before students arrive the next morning.

Janet Rubino, West Elementary, Great Falls, MT

This moon will help to light the way
To where I sit in school each day.
Bring it to open house tonight,
And give my jack-o'-lantern a light.

Lights, Camera, Action!

It's difficult to greet parents individually when they all arrive at one time. To help with this, create a video of a typical school day and have it playing continuously throughout open house. New arrivals will be attracted to it right away which can eliminate a line of parents waiting to speak to you. It's easier to make your video if you use a tripod. Start your video with a shot of your chalkboard that bears the message "Welcome to Our Class" along with the signature of each student. Then film each of your students entering your classroom and pausing in the doorway long enough to say, "Good morning!" As you tape typical events of the school day, your camera mounted on a tripod can record students working at a center, for instance, and your hands are free to take care of other matters. You'll know this video is a big hit when parents ask if they can get a copy.

Diane Hamilton, Travis Elementary School, Greenville, TX

This Is How You Do It, Dad

A neat way to encourage a meaningful open house experience is to plan for a night of cooperative-learning fun. A few days before open house, explain to children that they will be their parents' teachers and partners during their visit. When you greet a parent at the door, mention that he will find a folder of information and his child's work at the student's usual seat. Then point out that two centers have been indicated on the folder and that these are the centers that you would like for the family to participate in together. Also encourage families to select at least one other center of their choice to visit. Remind youngsters that they are to lead their parents through these activities. With this arrangement, parents get a good feel for classroom activities, students feel self-confident about having this responsibility, and you can make some observations regarding parent/child interactions.

Kathleen Ahern—Special Education, Skyline Elementary School, Stillwater, OK

Meet the Preschool Class

This bulletin board may be your most popular open house attraction. On the first day of school, photograph each child. Then interview him (or have an adult volunteer interview him) to get him to answer a few selected questions. Write the child's responses on an interview form containing the questions. When the child's picture is developed, have him attach it near the top of his interview form and decorate the bordering area as desired. Mount each youngster's interview form on a board with the title "Meet the Preschool Class." Adults will flock to this display to read the responses of their little ones and their classmates.

Sue Dier
Lincoln Community School
Lincoln, VT

What do you like to do best at school?
I like to build towers.

What do you like to do best at home?
I like to play outside.

The Pick of the Crop

If your newly enrolled preschoolers are invited to an open house, here's a way to get them involved right then and there. Decorate a bulletin board with a large apple-tree design. For each child, place a personalized apple cutout on a tabletop near the bulletin board. Also provide art supplies so that each child can decorate her apple. During open house, have each student attach her apple to the bulletin board apple tree with the help of her parent. When the evening is over, you'll be able to see at a glance which students were in attendance. The remaining youngsters may decorate and display their apples on the board when time permits.

Mary H. Case—Preschool, South Godwin Elementary School
Wyoming, MI

Masterful Invitations

Here's just the touch to spark each parent's interest in open house. First, enlarge and duplicate a class supply of the invitation on page 72. Then encourage each child to color a picture about school in the frame. Several days before open house, have each child take his invitation home and present it to his parent. Parents will enthusiastically anticipate open house when they see these invitations embellished with their own children's artistic masterpieces.

Sue De Riso
Barrington, RI

Every day I'm off to school,
And I think that's really cool!
But now it's time for you to see
This very special part of me!

Please come to open house on

Monday, October 18

So many different kinds of faces—
No two are exactly the same.
Find the one that's dear to you
That says, "I'm glad YOU came!"

Familiar-Face Find

Isn't it always nice to see a familiar face? Well, have your little ones create this clever collage to greet parents as they arrive for open house. In advance have each child cut out a supply of faces from old magazines. Encourage children to include plenty of diversity in the faces they choose. Then give each child a color copy of his school photo and have him cut his face out of it. Next, glue a copy of the poem shown in the center of a large piece of tagboard. During a center time, have each child, in turn, glue his face cutouts (including his own) around the poem. Then laminate the poster board and post the finished collage in a prominent position. Watch parents' faces light up as they pick their little ones' smiles out of the crowd. My, you look familiar to me!

Nan Hokanson, Circle Time Preschool
Sheboygan Falls, WI

You Ought to Be in Pictures!

On open house night, what could be more appealing to a parent than a poster-size picture of her child and her classmates? A couple of weeks before open house, take several pictures of your class. Consider photographing the class at various locations such as on a playground slide, while building with blocks in the block center, or while dressed in garb from your dramatic play area. After the pictures have been developed, select one to be enlarged, preferably to poster size. Just prior to open house, post the picture on your classroom door with the title "We've Got Class!"

Nina Tabanian, St. Rita School, Dallas, TX

"Tour-rific" Open House Idea

Give your little ones the pride of being classroom tour guides with this open house idea. Prepare a coloring sheet similar to the one shown that indicates key areas of interest in your classroom; then duplicate a copy for each child. When each child and her parent arrive at the open house, give them a copy of the sheet and a crayon. Direct the parent to ask his child to show him each listed area, having the child color in the corresponding space after they have spent some time together there. Everyone is sure to have a "tour-rific" time!

Ellen Bruno and Esta Fowler
Rio Rancho Elementary
Rio Rancho, NM

Open House

Making a List

You won't have to check twice to see if parents and their children enjoy your open house when you prepare this classroom checklist. Just prior to the event, ask your little ones to list those things or areas in your classroom that they would like for their parents to see. Record the items on a checklist; then duplicate a copy for each child's parent. As parents and children arrive, give them a checklist and encourage them to locate the listed items in your room. Take a look—there's lots to see in this special place!

Lucia Roney
Orange Park, FL

Welcome!
Our children would like for you to find

☑ the housekeeping center

☐ the hamster Maria brought to school

☐ our orange and blue paintings

Just for Dads

Sometimes men hesitate to mingle at open house when most of the participants are female. If this is the case with your students' parents, have a special Men's Night. Invite dads or other male role models to come to school one evening for an hour or so of school-related fun. Dads can participate in making nametags, playing circle and get-acquainted games, using centers, creating finger paintings or easel paintings, and building with blocks. Top off the evening with make-your-own sundaes and casual conversation.

Cheryl Songer—Pre/K
Wee Know Nursery School
Wales, WI

Little Red Schoolhouse

Take first-day-of-school photographs to use in these keepsakes that are the perfect open house treats for parents. Photograph each student in the classroom area that she likes the best; then have the pictures developed. For each student, cut a schoolhouse-shaped card similar to the one shown. Label the outside of the card "[Student's Name]'s First Day in Preschool." Attach the picture inside the card and add the date. Place the cards at students' seats so that parents can find them during open house. (Consider making a similar card in June for comparison.)

Ginger T. Davis
Florence Morris
W. Jesse Gurganus
Havelock, NC

Amanda's

First Day in Preschool

You're the Apple of My Eye

Invite parents and students to open house a few days before school begins. On the night of open house, photograph each youngster individually using a Polaroid camera. While you wait for each picture to develop, take a few minutes to get to know the family. Then staple the picture to a personalized apple cutout on a bulletin board tree. Once the youngsters are gone, you'll appreciate the fact that the display can help you put faces with names as you're working on first-week-of-school preparations. On the first day of school, each youngster will be eager to find his picture and to point it out to his new classmates.

Judy Graham—Preschool
Riverbend Preschool
Grand Rapids, MI

Christmas Open House

If your school is in the habit of having a Christmas program, consider switching to a Christmas open house. During this event, show parents a videotape of their children's recent activities. Also encourage parents to browse through displays of students' work and to sample student-made refreshments. In another area of the school, have Santa visit and pose for photographs with the children. This alternative to a Christmas program is more relaxing for both families and teachers, and it gives you an opportunity to chat informally with parents.

Terry Cochell—Director, Happytime Preschool, Canton, MO

Memorabilia Booklet

This idea works especially well with open houses that occur in mid-year or in the spring. Beginning on the first day of school, collect work samples, photos, and souvenirs of school activities for each student. Date each piece of memorabilia and file it away in a colorful file folder. For each child, also periodically record on a fill-in-the-blank form the date, his weight, and his height. Have each child answer a questionnaire just before you're ready to transform these bits and pieces into a memorabilia booklet. Record each student's responses and add this paper to the file. When it's time for open house, pull out each child's folder, glue odd-size pieces to sheets of paper, punch holes in the folder and papers, and fasten the pages between the folder covers using brads or plastic rings. Have each child illustrate the cover of his memorabilia booklet as he desires. This booklet idea never fails to please parents and students.

Denise Evans
Hodge Elementary
Denton, TX

Open House

Here's the Bus!

Bus-shaped folders, made and decorated by students, make terrific open house organizers. To make a bus-shaped folder, fold a 12" x 18" sheet of construction paper in half. Trim around the outer edge as indicated. Then use scissors to round off two small black construction paper squares for wheels, and glue them to the folder. Have each youngster draw and color kids and a bus driver on his bus, before filling the folder with completed papers.

Christy Owens
West Alexandria Elementary
West Alexandria, OH

Danny's Bus

Acting Up

Foster a strong home-school connection by going all out for open house. Have students plan and prepare invitations, decorations, refreshments, and artwork for the occasion. Encourage adult volunteers to dress as characters from children's literature for the event. On the night of the big event, have these costumed characters greet families, give directions or information when necessary, and serve refreshments. Have one character posted by the main exit so that each child can be given a treat before leaving and parents can be personally thanked for their attendance.

Sandy Wilke, Fort Dodge Cooperative Preschool, Fort Dodge, IA

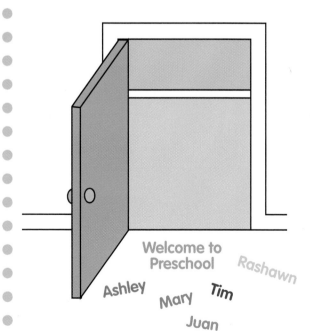

Welcome to Preschool
Rashawn
Ashley
Mary
Tim
Juan

Surprise Greetings

Welcome each child to open house before he even gets to the front door. Use sidewalk chalk to write the name of each of your students on the sidewalk near your entryway. Add simple drawings and a message of welcome.

Debbie Monts de Oca—Preschool

Look and see if you can find...

Bathroom Art easel Flag Books

Dolls and doll clothes Clothes, shoes, hats, and bags for dress-up Blocks Leader chart

Kitchen area Cubbies Puppets

Pictorial Scavenger Hunt

Here's a way to put anxious little ones at ease right away during open house. Make a look-and-find sheet that is made up of simple drawings or photocopied pictures of different areas of your classroom that you want youngsters to explore during open house. When families arrive, pass each child a copy of the sheet that you've prepared. Each family searches to find each of the pictured items and to explore the area once they've found the item. It's a great way to familiarize youngsters with their new classroom.

Chris Culen—Preschool Director
First Congregational Church Preschool
LaGrange, IL

Listen to This!

During the first few weeks of school, students learn many new songs, fingerplays, and poems. Many students go home singing and acting out the songs, but the parents can't always understand the words that their children are saying. To help with this, set up a listening center at open house featuring a tape of your little singers. In the center, parents may listen to recordings of your class singing their favorite songs. Offer to make a copy of the cassette for any parent who would like to supply a blank tape. Use this recording periodically in your listening center. Students will enjoy hearing themselves singing too.

Marie A. Sauvey, Jefferson School, Wauwatosa, WI

Follow Me, Mom!

If your youngsters have a set routine that they follow each morning which is prompted by prominently displayed picture cards, they're the perfect candidates for this suggestion. Prepare a set of picture cards that indicate the routine that students should follow for showing their parents around the classroom, ending with a greet-the-teacher card. When each family arrives, the youngster—having followed a similar routine prompted by picture cards on school day mornings—will go right to work showing parents around the classroom as indicated by the picture cards. What a boost to self-esteem it is for students to be responsible for giving their parents a classroom tour!

Marci Morris
Lampasas Primary School
Lampasas, TX

Dress up.

Build something.

Open House

Whose Mom Are You?

With all of the usual confusion of a big event like open house, it can be difficult to figure out which child belongs with which adult. To clarify family connections for yourself as well as for parents, make only one family's nametags from a color of construction paper and put identical stickers on each of the nametags belonging to that family. Use a different color and sticker design for each family represented.

Joan Adams—Preschool
Creative Learning Center
Montgomery, AL

Winter Holiday Open House

If you're considering a winter open house, why not have it in time to coincide with the winter holiday of your choice? In advance prepare a scavenger-hunt list that will take families around your classroom to discover different learning areas and to show them evidence of your recent areas of study. At the end of the list, word the directions so that families hunt for and enjoy student-made refreshments and so that children check their mailboxes to find treats from you. Provide each family with a copy of the list when they arrive at open house. Then send them off together to do each activity on the list. While parents and students are exploring, you're free to talk with others.

Diane Miesner—Pre/K, Rainbow Lane Preschool, Frohna, MO

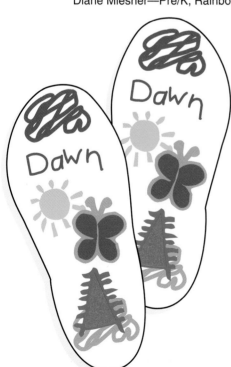

Matching Footprints

Several days before open house, interview each youngster to learn what his favorite classroom area/activity is. Assist each youngster in tracing and cutting out two identical sets of his footprints or shoeprints. Encourage him to decorate his footprints or shoeprints as desired. Then tape one set of footprints in the youngster's favorite classroom area or near the activity in which he most likes to participate. Put the other set of footprints in a labeled envelope. Display pictures showing each child participating in his favorite activity. On the night of open house, have each parent search the room to find a pair of footprints or shoeprints that match the ones in the envelope that you give him at the door. When a match is made, encourage the student to tell his parent about the favored area or activity and, if possible, engage the parent in some related learning fun.

Brona N. Smith
Arbor Ridge Elementary
Orlando, FL

Playground Pouch

Take along this playground pouch, and you'll be prepared for any minor boo-boos on the playground. Simply fill a fanny pack with tissues, adhesive bandages, baby wipes, disposable plastic gloves, and a zippered plastic bag for disposing of used tissues or wipes. Then strap the fanny pack around your waist when you take your class outdoors for recess. You'll be able to take care of little scratches and wipe away tears quickly so little ones can get back to having fun.

Bess McGrath—Pre-K
St. Rita School
Hamden, CT

Flag 'em In

Here's a high-flying alternative to blowing a whistle at the end of recess: Wave a special class flag! As each student notices the flag, she tells another child until all are lined up and ready to go. Add motivation to this process by allowing the first child to arrive to hold the flag. For more flag-watching incentive, have students help create the class flag by using fabric paint to make student handprints on a sheet of fabric. Sew a pocket narrow enough to securely hold a dowel in place; then slip the cloth over the dowel. Betsy Ross would be impressed!

Cheryl Kiser, Jackson Elementary, Boise, ID

Winter Dressing

Hung up on how to get all your little ones dressed to play in the frosty outdoors? Simply prepare a picture sequence of the necessary clothing; then display the pictures near your coat closet. Explain to the children to follow the order of the pictures when getting dressed for winter play. Youngsters will quickly learn that snow pants go on first, followed by boots, coats, hats, scarves, and mittens. All dressed? Let's go play!

Pam Waldrop—Preschool, Quality Care Child Care, Crown Point, IN

snowpants   boots   coat   hat   scarf   mittens

Zipper Chair

Do your little ones need an easy way to get help with their coat zippers? Try this adorable idea. Use fabric paint to paint a zipper on the front of a T-shirt. When the paint is dry, put the shirt over the back of a chair. (As an alternative, place a real coat with a zipper on the chair back.) Label the seat "Zipper Chair," and then cover the label with clear Con-Tact covering. Next, place the chair near your closet or the door. Encourage students to sit in the Zipper Chair when they encounter difficulty zipping up their jackets and coats to go outside. Or have a seat in the Zipper Chair and invite those children who need help to come to you. Zip 'em up and take 'em out!

Terry Steinke—Preschool
Emmaus Lutheran School
Indianapolis, IN

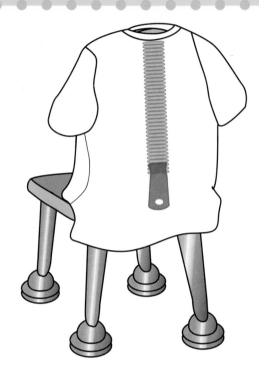

"1, 2, 3—That's Enough for Me!"

Do your youngsters linger at the water fountain after outdoor play? Speed things along with this simple rhyme. As each child takes her turn at the fountain, have the waiting children say, "1, 2, 3—that's enough for me!" The end of the rhyme is the drinker's signal that it's someone else's turn at the fountain.

Doris Porter—Preschool, Headstart, Anamosa, IA

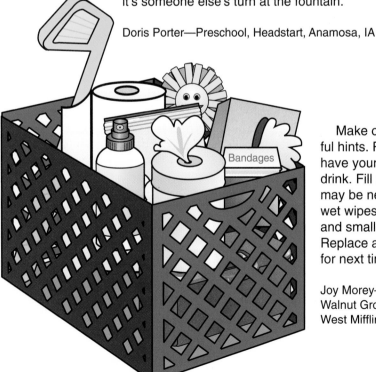

Outside Organization

Make outside play run like a charm with these helpful hints. Review safety rules before going outside, and have your youngsters use the restrooms and get a drink. Fill a milk crate or cardboard box with items that may be needed while you're outdoors (such as tissues, wet wipes, rubber gloves, a first-aid kit, a garbage bag, and small outside toys such as bubbles and chalk). Replace any items as you use them and you're ready for next time!

Joy Morey—Preschool
Walnut Grove Little House
West Mifflin, PA

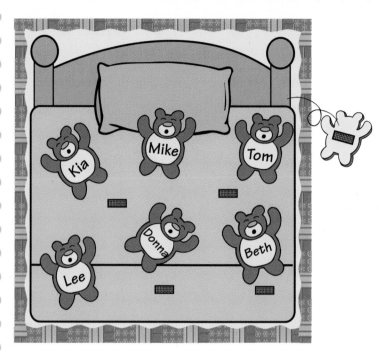

Did You Nap Today?

Encourage your little nappers to catch some z's with this fun incentive. At students' eye level, mount a laminated bed-shaped cutout on a wall of your room. Then mount a quilt-patterned border around the bed and attach a construction paper pillow cutout atop the bed. For each child, personalize a laminated teddy bear cutout. Cut one piece of self-adhesive Velcro fastener for each cutout. Attach the hook side of each Velcro piece to the back of a bear cutout. Mount the loop side of each piece on the bed cutout. Place the teddy bear cutouts on a table near the corner. Each day, after naptime, have each child who napped place his teddy bear on the bed. Parents can check the display each day to see if their children caught some z's!

Barb Young—Three-Year-Olds
Peace Memorial Child Care Center
Palos Park, IL

Naptime Boxes

Prepare these activity boxes for children who awaken from their naps early or who may not wish to sleep during your quiet rest time. If desired, cover several shoeboxes with colorful paper. Fill each box with items that can be played with independently and quietly, such as lacing cards, flannelboard pieces, or paper and crayons. A child may choose one of the boxes and take it back to his cot until rest time has ended.

Nancy Wolfgram—Four-Year-Olds, KinderCare Learning Center #1111, Lincoln, NE

A Napping Buddy

Enlist the help of a parent volunteer to make sure each of your youngsters has a warm and fuzzy impression of preschool. Using preprinted fabric pillow patterns (or your own designs) that resemble animals, make a soft, decorative pillow for each of your youngsters. When a child visits school for the first time, give him a pillow of his own to keep. With the animal pillow, provide a note (from the animal) that welcomes the child to school and says that it looks forward to being his napping buddy.

Hi! I'm your napping bud
When it's tim

Rest Time

Sleepy-Time Wand

Help your little ones relax into a state of sweet dreams with this rest-time wand. To make one, cut out two identical star shapes from tagboard. Brush one side of each star with glue; then sprinkle it with glitter. When the glue is dry, glue the stars together glitter sides out, leaving an opening in the bottom. Hot-glue an unsharpened pencil in the opening. During rest time use the wand to sprinkle imaginary pixie dust over the heads of your youngsters. Pleasant dreams!

Kristen Sharpe—Preschool
Kristen's Corner
Mansfield, MA

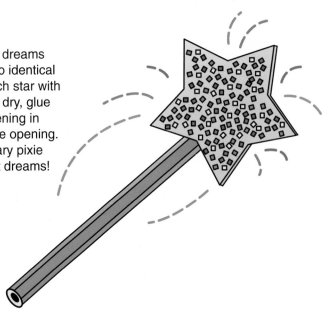

Nap Map

Your substitute or assistant will appreciate this naptime tip! Make a simple map of your classroom (by hand or computer); then laminate it. Use overhead transparency markers to draw the location of each child's nap mat. When you're out for the day, the naptime routine will go smoothly. If a new child enrolls or a child withdraws, simply change the map by erasing the necessary mats with a damp cloth.

Lee Marshall—Preschool
The Children's Council
Boone, NC

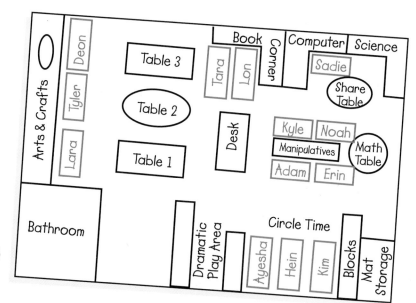

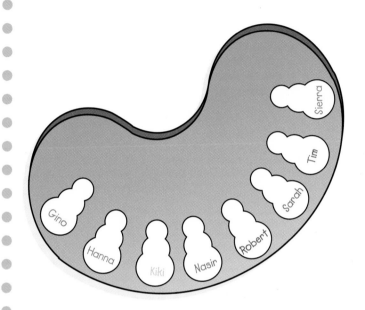

Easy Seating

Hey, preschool teachers! Manage your snacktime seating arrangements and teach name recognition at the same time. Here's how! Die-cut a class supply of shapes to reflect your current theme. Place the shapes on the tables so that you have a separate shape for each child. Cover the shapes with clear Con-Tact covering. Then use erasable markers to write a different child's name on each shape. During snacktime, have each child find her seat. After snack, just wipe the tables and the shapes clean. On your marks. Get set. Write! These nifty nametags are ready to use again!

Bobbi Albright—Three- and Four-Year-Olds
Day Care Services of Blair County/Leopold Center
Altoona, PA

Match Mates

Here's a management tip for seating at snacktimes and circle times that doubles as an opportunity to reinforce visual-discrimination skills. Prepare matching pairs of shapes for various seasons, holidays, and themes. For example, cut pairs of mitten shapes from wallpaper patterns, or similarly decorate pairs of heart cutouts. To use the match mates during a group time, place one shape in a matching pair at a seat or on the floor in your group area. Give the matching shape to a child. Direct each child to find his spot by finding his matching shape.

Susan Burbridge—Four-Year-Olds
Trinity Weekday School
San Antonio, TX

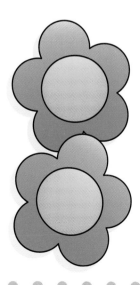

Snacktime

Place Cards

These place cards will not only help youngsters identify their names, but also will assist them in locating their seats at lunch or snacktime. To make a place card, cut a paper plate in half. Then cut the half-plate into a shape that corresponds with your current theme or unit. For example, if you are studying dinosaurs, you might cut the plate to resemble a stegosaurus. Have each child color or paint his shape. Next, fold the shape in half vertically so it will be freestanding. Write the child's name on each quadrant of the card. This organized method is a decorative way to seat your little ones.

Angela Lenz—Three-Year-Olds
Carriage House Children's Center
Pittsburgh, PA

Seating at Snacktime

Here's a simple method for seating students at snack- or mealtime. In advance, place different colored stick-on dots, stickers, or shape cutouts on a classroom supply of jug lids. Mount matching dots, stickers, or cutouts on small pieces of tagboard; then laminate the tagboard if desired. Tape each piece of tagboard on a different chair around your snack table. Each day, when it's snack- or mealtime, have each child choose a jug lid from a container; then have him locate the chair with the matching piece of tagboard. Using this method will allow youngsters to socialize with different classmates each day.

Sherry L. Petrik, Love And Tender Care, Dell Rapids, SD

Milk or Juice?

If your students get to choose a beverage for snacktime, try this idea to help make selections run like a charm. In advance, collect one half-pint carton for each of the following: white milk, chocolate milk, and juice. Cut the top off each carton. Mount each carton on a wall at students' eye level. Program each child's name on an individual craft stick, and place the sticks on a nearby shelf or table. Every morning, as each child comes into the room, have him find his stick and place it in the beverage container of his choice. Using this timesaver, you'll be able to see at a glance your students' drink choices.

Brenda Wells And Donna Cook
Roseland Park Elementary
Picayune, MS

Snack Reminder

Being prepared for snacktime is a cinch with a snack basket. To make a snack basket, decorate a basket with colorful plastic or rubber food items such as fruits, vegetables, and cookies. At the end of each week, select a child to take the snack basket home. Ask the child's family to fill the basket with enough snacks for the following week and return the basket to school on Monday. This idea will prevent losing written reminders, and the children will just eat it up!

Mrs. Andy King—Preschool
Hope Creative Preshool
Winter Haven, FL

Snacktime Tip

Plastic bowls make snacktime cleanup quick and easy! Before serving snacks, place a large plastic bowl in the center of each table. After he finishes his snack, ask each youngster to place his trash in the bowl. Then have helpers empty the bowls into the trash can and wipe them out. Cleanup is a snap!

Sheila Weinberg, Warren Point School, Fair Lawn, NJ

Personalized Placemats

These personalized placemats will help you organize snacktime in a snap. Cut half as many vinyl placemats in half vertically as there are children in your class. For each child, attach a strip of masking tape to a placemat half; then label the tape with the child's name and any food allergies. These placemats look spiffy, and they wipe clean in a jiffy!

Lee Turner—Two- and Three-Year-Olds
Chamblee Methodist Kindergarten
Chamblee, GA

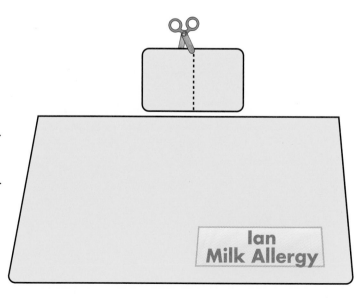

Ian
Milk Allergy

Transitions and Time Fillers

The Waiting Tree
Ever need a tool for helping your children wait patiently? Make a waiting tree, and you'll have just what you need at your fingertips! To prepare, locate a large potted plant or secure a branch in a pot. Cut out a supply of seasonal or thematic paper shapes. On each shape, write a different activity suggestion that requires only a few minutes to complete. For example, you could include a game of Simon Says, the words to a favorite song, several what-if questions, and a story starter. Attach a short yarn loop to each shape, and then hang it on the plant or branch. When you find yourself with short, unplanned time, just choose a shape off the waiting tree and follow the suggestion written on it. Time flies when you're having fun!

Cindy Lawson—Toddler/Preschool
Certified Family Daycare
Shell Lake, WI

Once upon a time there was a busy bee. He flew…

Magic Number
Improvise with this math game when you've got a few minutes between activities. Write a number on a scrap of paper. Fold the paper and attach it to your blackboard with a magnet. Beneath the magnet draw and number a number line. Ask your youngsters to guess the magic number that you have written on the paper. When a number is guessed, circle it on the number line; then tell youngsters whether the magic number is higher or lower than (greater than or less than) the number guessed. Continue marking students' guesses on the number line until the magic number is called. Unfold the paper to confirm that the number is correct. Children enjoy trying to guess the number with as few guesses as possible.

Mona Nale, Evergreen Elementary, Midlothian, VA

Deanna D…
Richard C…
Amber Burbridge
123 Anywhere St.
Wrens, GA
333-555-1234

Birthday: June 26

Personal Information
Have a few minutes to spare? Why not use the time to review personal information such as addresses, phone numbers, or birth dates. So that you'll always be prepared to use this activity as a time filler, keep a copy of each youngster's emergency card in an easily accessible notebook or on a prominently displayed ring. Then ask each youngster to name one bit of personal information (such as her birthdate) in turn. Soon youngsters will be committing this information to memory, and you'll delight in seeing that classmates can often assist students who are having difficulty with this skill.

Annette Shuman
Wrens Elementary
Wrens, GA

Transitions and Time Fillers

Traffic Light

Make transition times easier with this traffic-light display. To prepare the display, cut five circles from construction paper—one each from red, yellow, and green, and two from black. Glue the red, yellow, and green circles to a large, black construction paper rectangle to resemble a traffic light. Label each of the three circles to reflect important segments of your school day. For instance, label the red circle "Quiet Time," the yellow circle "Cleanup Time," and the green circle "Activity Time." Laminate the traffic light and the two black circles. Post the display in a prominent location. Use Sticky-Tac to cover two of the colored circles with the black circles. During transition times, a change in the color visible will indicate a change in the classroom activity.

Noelle Leung—Preschool
Arlington, MA

Could You Explain That?

During a few extra minutes, have youngsters take turns explaining how things are done. In advance, label a set of cards with "how to [activity]." For example, label cards "how to make a cake," "how to wash a car," and "how to brush your teeth." Then when the opportunity presents itself, have youngsters take turns drawing a card from the deck and explaining the corresponding process in detail. It's a great way to improve language skills.

Jo Ann Moore, Nancy Hart Elementary, Hartwell, GA

Musical Names

This version of Musical Chairs will help youngsters recognize their names as well as aid in transitional times. Prepare a name card for each child. Arrange a class supply of chairs in a circle; then place a name card on each chair. Play as you would Musical Chairs, having each child sit on the chair with her name card when the music stops. As you remove a chair each round, have the child whose seat was taken move on to the next activity, such as washing her hands or preparing to go outside. Rearrange the name cards on the chairs before each round. Everyone's a winner in this game!

Gina Mahony—Preschool
Children's Preschool Workshop
Barrington, IL

Transitions and Time Fillers

Toll-Free Calls

For this productive activity, you'll need two telephones. Place both phones in plain view. Then punch out a child's home telephone number, calling out each number as you press it. Hold the receiver to your ear while waiting for a response. The child whose number you called should answer the other phone. If no one answers, explain that the line must be busy and that you'll call again. If the child does answer, say, "Hello," and exchange a few pleasantries before hanging up and calling another child.

Joan Adams—Preschool
Creative Learning Center
Montogomery, AL

Categories

Bolster your youngsters' classification skills with a spur-of-the-moment game called Categories. Name (or have a student name) a category such as things found at the beach, things that fly, things you eat for breakfast, or things to wear in the winter. Each child, in turn, names an appropriate item, avoiding items that have already been mentioned. If desired, each child may line up or move to another area of the room when he has taken his turn.

Kathy Agnello—Preschool, First Presbyterian Preschool, Jackson, MI

What's Your Position?

Have your youngsters practice position concepts when you finish up a little early. Place a chair at the front of the room. Then select a student and direct him to crawl under, climb over, and stand behind the chair. Have him select a youngster to have the next turn. Ask this child to sit on, stand in front of, and lie beneath the chair. Continue in this manner using a variety of position words.

Lenora Norris
Norcross Elementary
Suwanee, GA

Transitions and Time Fillers

Roly-Poly Portraits

Prepare these picture cubes and you'll roll right into games and transitions! Obtain a plastic picture cube for every six children in your class. Personalize a photo of each child. Insert a different child's photo into each side of each cube. (As an alternative, glue photos to the sides of empty mug gift boxes.) Use the picture cubes to work on classmate recognition or name recognition. Or roll the cubes to assign jobs and centers. When playing games, roll the cube to determine whose turn it is. With these ideas, you're on a roll!

Ginette M. Harvey and Traci Kilbreath—Three-, Four-, and Five-Year-Olds
Portage County Integrated Preschool
Aurora, OH

Dreamin'

This is one active option your youngsters will certainly prefer. To start the activity, have each youngster lie down on a carpeted area and be very still. Then say, "I had a dream, and in my dream, I was a [name an animal or a machine]." When the animal or machine is named, encourage everyone to move as it would move. Then have students lie still again and select a child to be the next dreamer. Continue in this matter until each child has had an opportunity to name the object in the dream. End the activity by saying, "I had a dream. And when I woke up, I was just me."

Shelley Hansen—Preschool, Wichita State University Child Development Center, Wichita, KS

Ball Toss

It only takes a few minutes every now and then to help youngsters improve their catching and throwing skills. So when you have a few minutes, have youngsters stand in a circle and toss an inflated ball back and forth. If you're trying to keep the noise level down, you may want to ask that children toss the ball without making noise. No doubt they'll have a ball as they're improving their gross-motor skills.

Barbara Moffatt, George's Creek School
Lonaconing, MD

Transitions and Time Fillers

Song Bag

While this bag is not a bag of tricks, once you use it a few times, you'll think you've found the real trick for filling spare time. Decorate a drawstring fabric bag with musical notes. Then each time your youngsters learn a new song, have a child draw a picture clue for the song on a card. Write the name of the song on the card and place it in the bag. Hang the song bag where it can easily be reached. Then, whenever you have the time, reach for the bag and have a student draw a card. Sing the song as a group; then have another youngster choose another card from the bag.

Debbie Damron
Ellington Elementary School
Glendora, CA

Baa, Baa, Black Sheep

Mystery Person

Here's a five-minute filler that will bring out the deductive-reasoning abilities and observation skills of each of your little detectives. Begin by asking five students to stand at the front of the room. Secretly select one of the children to be the mystery person. Proceed to give the class hints about the mystery person. Include clues that mention the child's physical characteristics (hair color, for example) and descriptions of his clothing. Each time a clue is given that rules out a child in the lineup, encourage detectives to ask for that child to be seated, since he must not be the mystery person. Continue giving clues until only the mystery person remains standing. Why will your youngsters ask for this game again and again? It's elementary, my dear Watson.

Susan Barr—Pre-First, Narragansett Elementary School, Narragansett, RI

Quick Draw Letter

You're never seen such enthusiasm as your youngsters will exude during this race-the-teacher game. Before starting the game, label a score box "teacher" and "students." Explain to students that if they can name the letter or number you're writing on the board before you finish writing it, they'll get the point. Conversely, if you finish writing the letter before anyone names it, you'll get the point. Then select a letter or number at random and write it on the board. The students will almost always win the race. But even better than that, they win because they know the letters and numbers so well.

Debbie Benedict
Black Hawk Elementary
Waterloo, IA

Transitions and Time Fillers

The Picture Box

Some youngsters may find themselves with time to spare, even though others are occupied. Use this suggestion, and youngsters will know that they can always go to the picture box to fill a few minutes. Keep a box filled with a variety of laminated magazine pictures. When a youngster has some time on his hands, he may select a picture from the box and tell a friend, or you, about it.

Cherly L. Bailey
Penns Manor Elementary School
Clymer, PA

Chime Time

Smooth out transition-time turmoil with this musical idea. Ring a small wind chime to quietly signal transitions. The results will be music to your ears!

Michelle Espelien—Preschool, St. James Preschool, Burnsville, MN

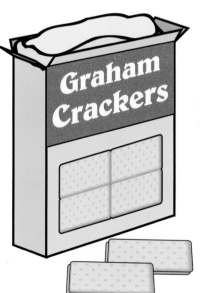

Tasty Transition

Boost your youngsters' brainpower for an upcoming activity by treating them to a snack during a few minutes of downtime. Keep some graham crackers or Teddy Grahams snacks on hand for this purpose. You'll be surprised at the significant boost this may give your youngsters as they start the next activity.

Beverly Bippes
Humphrey Public School
Humphrey, NE

Transitions and Time Fillers

Exercise Club

Here's a fun way to help your youngsters release energy and fill a few minutes between lessons or activities. Prepare for this activity in advance by making an exercise cube. To make one, cut the tops off two half-gallon milk or juice cartons so that the cartons are about four inches tall. Push one carton bottom inside the other to form a cube. Color illustrations of six exercises, or use an instant camera to photograph a youngster doing each of six exercises. Attach each of these illustrations or photographs to a side of the cube before covering the cube with clear Con-Tact covering. To begin the activity, select (or have a child select) a number less than ten. Then have a child roll the cube. Whatever exercise is faceup when the cube lands is the exercise that youngster will do. The number that has been previously selected indicates the number of repetitions of the exercise. Play continues as time permits, with children taking turns rolling the cube.

Jan Clark
Washington School
Livonia, MI

Busy Bodies

Use this rhythm activity to keep little bodies busy while waiting in line. Perform a movement for children to imitate, such as clapping. After a while, change to another movement such as head nodding. Then let students take turns selecting and leading the activity. No more fidgeting in line!

Sherri S. McWhorter—Pre-K, Franklin County Head Start, Carnesville, GA

Sing-Along

Even when you don't have a few minutes between lessons, a sing-along is the type of thing youngsters will be begging for. To prepare for those times that you can squeeze in a song, poem, or fingerplay, make a booklet for each of your major themes. Then whenever you find a song, poem, or fingerplay that you'd like to share with your youngsters, photocopy it and insert the photocopy into the corresponding booklet. You'll be amazed at how often you'll return to these collections for five-minute fillers.

Monica D. Phillips
Harvard Elementary
Houston, TX

Transitions and Time Fillers

What Do You Know?

Everyone will be amazed at how this stack of knowledge grows through the year! Begin by labeling a recipe box "What Do You Know?" At the end of each week, write questions that are relevant to that week's studies on index cards. Then put the cards in the box. When you need a five-minute filler, take the stack of cards from the box and ask children questions from the cards. Each subsequent time that you remove the stack of cards, emphasize how the stack is growing! At the end of the year, use the cards to highlight how much everyone has learned. Wow—look how much you know!

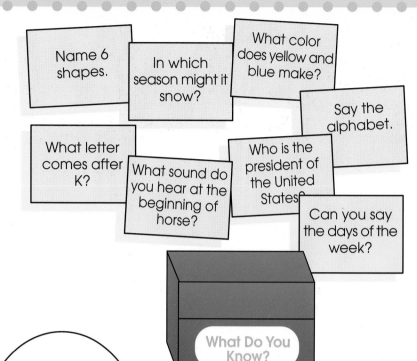

Five-Minute Filler

Need a time filler for those extra minutes during the day? Keep the ball rolling in your classroom with this skill-reinforcement idea. Seat your youngsters in a circle. Roll a sponge ball to a student. Then ask him a review question about the first letter of his name, the beginning sound of a word, or the color of an object. Continue in this manner by rolling the ball to another student. This fun-filled activity is certain to keep everyone on the ball.

Lynn Cadogan
Starkey Elementary
Seminole, FL

Transitions and Time Fillers

What's Missing

Keep your flannelboard and flannelboard cutouts handy for this transitional activity. Place a few cutouts on your flannelboard. Give youngsters an adequate amount of time to note the cutouts displayed. Then turn the board around so that youngsters can't see what you're doing and remove one cutout from the flannelboard. When you again show youngsters the display, have them name the missing cutout. Increase the difficulty level of this activity, if desired, by rearranging the cutouts on the flannelboard after removing a cutout.

Mrs. Thomas M. Ellison
Myers Park Presbyterian Weekday School
Charlotte, NC

Musical Button

Signal to youngsters when center time is over and it's time to move quietly to the next activity. Purchase a musical button (the kind that is sometimes sewn in a doll) from a craft store. Tell students that each day when center time is over, the musical button will sound. On this cue, have students move quietly into position for their next activity. Choose a student who cleaned his center quietly, and write his name on the blackboard. This student will have the honor of pushing the button after center time the next day.

Connie Crocker—Substitute Teacher, Goose Creek School District, Baytown, TX

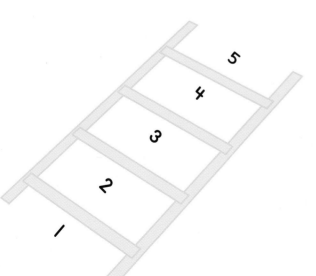

Transition Train

All aboard the transition train for a fun way to teach youngsters to line up! Use masking tape to create a railroad track on the floor in the area where students line up, making sure the track is long enough for each child to have her own space. During transition time, direct each child to stand in her own space on the track.

To make a transition time into a learning opportunity, add different-colored geometric shapes, letters, or numbers to the spaces in the track. Cover them with clear Con-Tact covering for durability. Also consider creating matching picture cards. Then, during transitions, show each child a picture card and have her find and stand on the matching space. All aboard for transition fun!

Melissa Nelson
St. Nicholas School
Zanesville, OH

Transitions and Time Fillers

Guessing Game

Here's a fun and productive way to fill a few minutes. Prepare for this activity in advance by making or locating a set of picture cards. Begin play by drawing a picture card from the deck and concealing it from the students. Give a series of descriptions for the object without saying what it is. The first youngster to correctly identify the picture on the card may draw a card and give the descriptions for the next round of play.

T. M. Hanak—Preschool
Linden Little Rascals
Linden, MI

It lives on a farm and says "neigh!"

Choose a nursery rhyme for the class to recite.

All It's Cracked Up to Be

Break out of your usual time-filling modes with this attractive transition activity. In advance, write each of several different task on slips of paper. Place each task slip inside a plastic egg. Then place the eggs in a basket and top them with a stuffed toy hen or rabbit. When you've got time to spare, have a youngster select an egg and complete the task inside. Oh boy, Sam, your task is to choose a nursery rhyme for the class to recite!

Linda Tecler—Preschool
Georgetown Hill Child Care Center
Potomac, MD

Transitions and Time Fillers

Seasonal Selections

Plan ahead to give your time-filling activities a seasonal flair. During February, for example, fill a mailbox with heart-shaped cutouts, each of which has been labeled with an impromptu task. Your March activities may be presented in a black plastic cauldron filled with shiny gold coin cutouts that have been programmed with tasks. When you have minutes to spare, have youngsters take turns drawing cutouts from the container and completing the tasks selected. Keyana, your cutout says "Choose a song for the class to sing."

Chris Garchow—Pre-K
St. Paul's Lutheran School
Janesville, WI

Higgety, Biggety Bumblebee

Can you say your name for me? This catchy rhyme draws the attention of your linguistic and auditory youngsters while the movement keeps those kinesthetic kids involved. To begin, seat students in a circle. Say the rhyme below; then toss a soft ball or beanbag to a child. Ask that child to say his name. As abilities permit, encourage the whole class to repeat that name, whisper that name, clap the syllables, and say the beginning sound. Then say the rhyme again, asking the child who is currently holding the ball to toss it to another child when the rhyme has been said. Continue in the same manner until each child's name (and yours!) has been said.

Higgety, biggety bumblebee—
Can you say your name for me?

Melissa Jackson, Miano School, Los Banos, CA

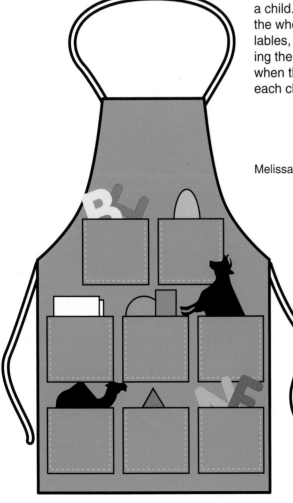

Learning Apron

When you find yourself with a little too much class time on your hands, make a run for your apron. Yes, your apron. In advance, sew extra pockets on an apron and decorate it as desired. Fill the apron pockets with letter or number cutouts for youngsters to identify, items related to nursery rhymes to stimulate choral nursery-rhyme telling, or index cards with questions relating to students' likes and dislikes. Have youngsters take turns picking your pockets and responding to the items pulled from your apron pockets. "Manuel, you pulled a blackbird from your pocket. What nursery rhyme do you know that has one or more blackbirds in it? Let's say that rhyme together!"

Heidi Lynnette Johnson—Pre-K
First Class Day Care
Port Richey, FL

Transitions and Time Fillers

Interviews

Keep an inexpensive microphone handy, and you can do this activity at a moment's notice. When time permits, interview a student while holding the microphone. After he has shared some interesting things that have happened to him recently, interview someone else. This is Elaine Edwards reporting for TALK NEWS. Back to you, Bob.

Elaine Edwards
Stanley Switlik Elementary
Marathon, FL

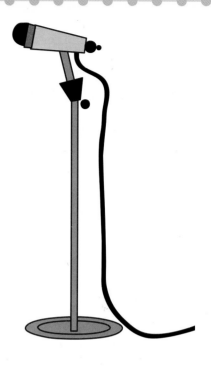

Silly Alphabet Song

Fill a few minutes with this version of the ABC song. Seat your youngsters in a large circle. Have youngsters join in as you sing the ABC song. Then select a child to name the first letter of his name. Sing the ABC song again, but when you reach the child's first initial, have everyone slap his hand over his mouth and pause. The selected child then points to his first initial on an alphabet chart and the song resumes. Continue as long as time permits or until each child has had a turn.

Robyn Rochman—Preschool, Castehill County Day School, Tucson, AZ

Being the Teacher

Have a little extra time? Select a youngster to pretend to be the teacher for a few minutes. You can sit back and observe as he uses a pointer to point to numbers, letters, and colors for his classmate to identify. Not only is this a quick review, but it's also a great self-esteem booster for the youngster who gets to be the teacher.

Mrs. Andy King—Preschool
Hope Creative Preschool
Winter Haven, FL

Transitions and Time Fillers

Body-Part Challenge

Grins and giggles will abound during this transitional activity that focuses on parts of the body. Have each youngster touch a specified part of his body to another specified part. For example, ask students to touch their toes to their ears or their elbows to their heels. It's not hard to imagine the fun youngsters will have with these and other similar tasks. Not only does this activity increase your youngsters' knowledge of body parts, but it's also a sure mood elevator!

Sandy Bertschy
Sugar Creek Elementary
Bentonville, AR

Mirroring

Here's a totally quiet time filler that's like Follow the Leader. Instruct youngsters to mimic your actions. Then pose in a series of zany positions, moving from one pose to another without pausing. Continuous eye contact and unstoppable smiles make this transition activity a fun-filled diversion.

Sandy Bertschy

Roll and Count

This transition activity is great counting practice and exercise. In advance, locate a pair of large foam-rubber dice. Then when time permits, select a child to toss the dice. He may count the total number of dots or add the numbers represented by both dice. When the sum of the dice has been identified, have the child choose an exercise or movement that can be done that number of times. If the sum of the dice was six, for example, he could do six jumping jacks along with his classmates.

Sherry Griffin
Hester School
Farmersville, CA

I'm so glad ＿＿＿＿＿＿＿＿＿＿＿＿＿＿＿
(child's name)

is in my class!

＿＿＿＿＿＿＿＿＿＿＿＿＿＿＿＿＿＿＿
(teacher's signature)

©The Education Center, Inc. • *500 Classroom Tips* • TEC60846

Car Pattern
Use with "A Smooth Ride" on page 158.

©The Education Center, Inc. • *500 Classroom Tips* • TEC60846

Invitation

Use with "Masterful Invitations" on page 44.

Every day I'm off to school,
And I think that's really cool!
But now it's time for you to see
This very special part of me!

Please come to open house on

Parent Note

Use with "Topic Trackers" on page 180.

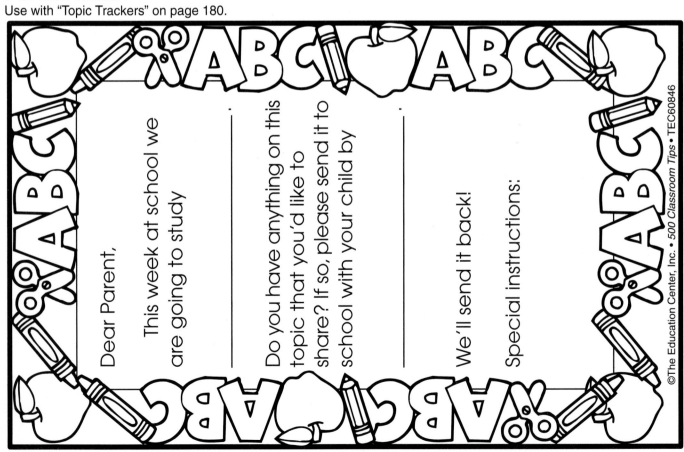

Dear Parent,

This week at school we are going to study

Do you have anything on this topic that you'd like to share? If so, please send it to school with your child by

We'll send it back!

Special instructions:

Contents

Bulletin Boards and Displays

Borders Galore

Do you have borders galore? Try this tip for organizing your borders and more. Organize your borders and items such as rolls of stickers by theme or season; then arrange them on extension rods. Position the rods between the walls of a storage closet. Now when you're ready to use these supplies, you'll only have to pull out what you need.

Annette Horton—PreK
Frederick Douglass Elementary
Winchester, VA

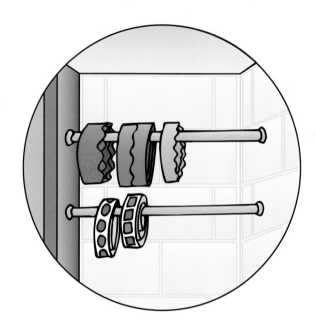

Run for the Border

Run to get your next few months' worth of bulletin board border; then make use of this timesaving tip! As you prepare your next bulletin board, choose a neutral background; then layer and attach several borders for future planned displays. For example, mount a Christmas border, then cover it with a Halloween border, and finally top both of those with a fall border. When it's time to change the display, simply peel off the top layer of border. The next border is in place and ready to use!

Amy Barsanti—Four-Year-Olds, St. Andrew's Preschool, Nags Head, NC

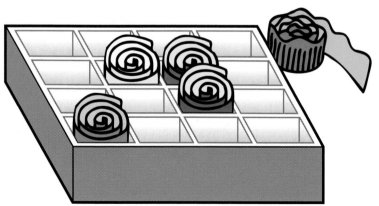

No More Border Clutter!

Feeling like you want to run from the border clutter created by the rolls of bulletin board borders in your closet or drawers? Here's a tip for you! If your school orders large amounts of crayons or markers that come in a divided box, save the box when the supplies are distributed. Then put your rolls of borders in the divided sections. The rolls stay neat, and they are easily accessible too!

Claudia Johnson—Preschool, Special Education
New Kent Primary
New Kent, VA

A Perfect Fit

Here's a timesaver for bulletin board decorating. Assign a number to each bulletin board in your classroom. When you remove the border from one of your boards, attach a slip of paper labeled with that board's number to the roll or gathered strips of border. When you want to put the border up again, you'll know which board it's been cut to fit.

Rita H. McClain
Harris Elementary School
Forest City, NC

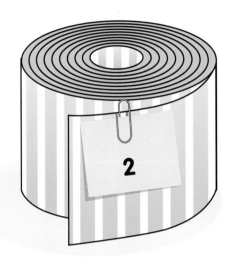

Beautiful Bulletin Boards

Your bulletin boards will look appealing all year long when you back them with neutral-colored wallpaper before adding your display pieces. Wallpaper is durable, and its color won't fade. With this method you'll save time, and your bulletin boards will look great display after display.

Susan Dzurovcik—Preschool, Valley Road School, Clark, NJ

Bulletin Board Storage

If keeping track of all the pieces of your bulletin board sets is a challenge, try this nifty idea. Using wide, clear tape, mount a manila envelope to the back of a large cutout of one of your bulletin board sets. Place the smaller parts of the set (such as letters or manipulative pieces) inside the envelope. Attach a photo of the completed bulletin board to the envelope for a quick and convenient reference.

MaryBeth Schlender
Christian Chapel Day Care
Onalaska, WI

Alphabetical Order

Try this handy organizational method for quick access to your precut bulletin board letters. Insert a set of alphabet-tabbed index cards into a 4" x 6" index-card or recipe-card storage box. Then sort and file the letters into their correct divisions. No more wasted time going through mounds of mixed-up letters. Captions are ready in a flash!

Janice Lagard—Three- and Four-Year-Olds
Discovery Years
Hamburg, NJ

Display Saver

Try this idea to keep Sticky-Tac from leaving greasy spots on favorite visuals and letter cutouts that are not laminated. Put pieces of transparent tape on the back of the visuals; then attach the Sticky-Tac to the tape. The tape stops the moisture from penetrating through to the front of the visuals. It also helps keep the visuals from tearing when it's time to remove them from the wall. Now that's a mint of a hint!

Renee Culver—PreK
Rogys Gingerbread House
Peoria, IL

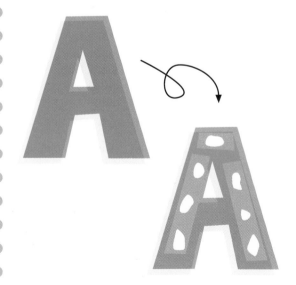

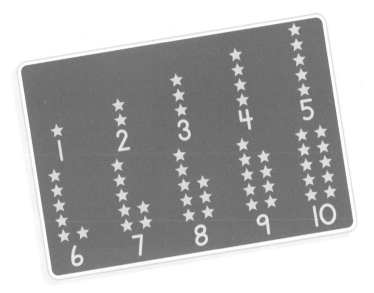

Easy-Care Decorating

Hey, toddler teachers! Do you find that the posters in your classroom are not as long-lived as you would like? Try this unique idea for decorating your room's walls. Use double-sided tape to mount children's educational picture placemats to your walls, making sure that the placemats are at toddlers' eye level. These vinyl mats are sturdy and can be easily wiped clean. Now you have long-lasting and educational decorating at their fingertips!

Judy Tanzone—Toddlers
Harmony School
Princeton, NJ

Space-Saving Chart Holder

Need more wall space? Then use your classroom door and a pair of wreath hangers to create instant chart holders. Simply place two wreath hangers on your door. Attach a pipe cleaner loop to each hole on the chart and then hang each loop from a separate hanger. What a great way to save space!

Sarah Booth—PreK
Messiah Nursery School
South Williamsport, PA

Bulletin Boards and Displays

Extra Display Space

If tape and other adhesives just won't stick to your classroom wall, try this colorful display technique. Sew a ¾-inch casing at one end of a two-yard length of colorful fabric. Insert a ½-inch dowel through the casing. Suspend the resulting banner from the ceiling; then pin on desired items for an eye-catching display.

Betty P. Reynolds
Stewartsville Elementary
Vinton, VA

Laminating Film Leftovers

Get two uses from one material with this clever idea. When cutting out laminated visuals, save those excess pieces of laminating film. Trim off the unruly edges and use the film pieces with your overhead projector. The film works just as well as an overhead transparency, so turn that trash into a real treasure!

Linda Dean—PreK, P. E. E. P., Beulaville, NC

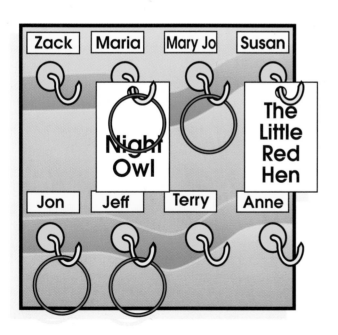

Cup Hook Display

A display with cup hooks can have multiple uses in your classroom! To make this display board, paint or stain a piece of plywood. Every few inches, screw a cup hook into the plywood. Write each child's name on a separate strip of construction paper or labeling tape. Then attach one child's name above each cup hook. Use the cup hook display for taking attendance. For example, as each child enters the room, have him place a ring (the seal from a milk jug) on his hook. Another timesaving way to use this display is to make a card for each book in your class library. Punch a hole near the top of each card. When a student checks out a book, have him hang the corresponding card on his hook. One quick glance at the board will tell you which students have checked out books.

Jan Prince
Booth Elementary School
Enfield, IL

Yarn Displays

Do you get all strung out over displays that just won't stick to the walls? If so, put away your tape and try using yarn instead. In compliance with fire safety codes, tie lengths of yarn to hooks mounted near the ceiling. Using clothespins, attach student work along the pieces of yarn. Not only will the work stay in place, but the vertical arrangement makes an interesting display.

Marcia Longo
Hancock North Central Elementary, Pass Christian, MS

Bulletin Board Album

Keep a picture-perfect record of bulletin board ideas in a photo album. Each time you decorate a bulletin board, photograph the results. Also photograph other favorite displays that you see around your school and other schools that you visit. Organize the resulting photographs in a photo album. To enhance your collection, cut out bulletin boards featured in teacher magazines. The next time you're searching for that perfect display, you'll have an album full of good ideas to choose from!

Gayla Hammer
West Elementary and South Elementary, Lander, WY

Storing Letter Cutouts

Here's a tip for organizing your bulletin board letters. Sort letters by style, size, and/or color; then place each group of letters in a gallon-size, resealable plastic storage bag. Three-hole-punch the plastic bags as shown and place them in a three-ring notebook. Store the binder in a handy location. The next time you need letter cutouts, you'll have them neatly organized and ready to use!

Angela Virostick
West Hill Elementary
Sharon, PA

Poem and Flannelboard File

Keep your poems and flannelboard pieces right at your fingertips with this convenient storage system. Each time you use a poem, make a small copy of it to mount on an index card. Place the index card in a labeled envelope with corresponding flannelboard pieces. File the envelopes by theme, season, or holiday in a file box. Your organized poems and flannelboard pieces are readily available whenever you need them.

Liz Mooney
Rayne, LA

Humpty Dumpty

Weekday Files

End those paper pileups with this quick and easy filing system. Label each of five different-colored file folders with a day of the week. Store all papers, books, and other materials needed for a particular day in the appropriate folder. Then all you (or your substitute) need is your daily folder and you're ready to go!

Terry Schreiber
Holy Family School
Norwood, NJ

Awards/Rewards File

Keep your awards and certificates right at your fingertips with this handy organizational idea. Make a file folder for each award or certificate that you plan to use. Identify each award file by coloring one copy of each award and gluing it to the front of the folder. Laminate the folder and place the original award inside along with several copies. The awards are sorted and ready for giving.

Debra S. Bott
Duson Elementary
Duson, LA

A Box of Ideas

Update the ideas in this file to keep pace with your youngsters' developing skills. Program each divider of an expanding file folder with a different time to match the segments of your daily schedule. Behind each divider, place a card or cards that detail what is to be done during that period of time. Throughout the year, whenever you see a neat idea, jot it down on a card and place it in one of the time slots in your file. Use a paint pen to clearly mark the file so that the substitute teacher will see it right away. Not only is this a great way to supply her with ideas, but in a pinch you can pull an idea from the file to fill a five-minute gap.

Joan Adams
Creative Learning Center
Montgomery, AL

Nametags

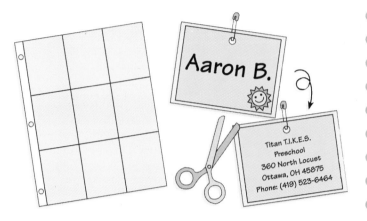

Nifty Nametags

Do away with torn and tattered nametags with this nifty idea. Cut clear, plastic, three-ring binder pages used to display baseball cards into nine individual pockets each. For each nametag, cut a 3½" x 2½" rectangle of construction paper. Print a child's name on the rectangle; then attach decorative stickers if desired. (If the nametags are to be used on field trips, consider putting the child's name on one side of the tag and the school's name and phone number on the other side.) Slide the paper into the pocket. Punch a hole in the top of the pocket. Using a large safety pin, attach the nametag to the child's clothing. For trips, pin the nametags on with the school name showing. (Public safety officers believe that labeling a child with his name can work to the advantage of a would-be abductor.)

Brenda Berger—Three-, Four-, and Five-Year-Olds
Titan T.I.K.E.S. Preschool
Ottawa, OH

A Spot for You

Personalize each child's spot at a table by making these seasonal nametags. Glue a child's picture to a cutout or decorative notepad page labeled with the child's name. Then use clear Con-Tact covering to adhere the nametag onto the table at the child's assigned space. If desired, prepare a matching nametag to use to label the child's cubbie. Here's a spot just for you!

Chrissy Casey—Preschool, Rocking Horse Child Care Center
Malvern, PA

Handsome Nametags

Your little ones will be happy to lend you a hand when making these self-adhering nametags for your tables or cubbies. To make a nametag, cut a square of clear Con-Tact covering that is slightly larger than a child's hand. Remove the backing from the square. Have a child press her hand into tempera paint, then onto the adhesive side of the Con-Tact covering. When the paint is dry, press the square onto a tabletop or the child's cubby; then use a permanent marker to write the child's name below her handprint. What a nifty nametag!

Carolyn Macdonald—Four-Year-Olds
Kiddie Haven Day Care
Brockton, MA

Free Nametags

Ask parents who attend seminars and conventions to save the plastic pin-on name-tags that they receive. Collect enough for the largest class in your school. Then, when a class is ready to go on a field trip, that teacher can program a class supply of sheets to slide into the nametags. Multiple classes can use the tags over and over again!

Joy Wallace—Preschool, Home Daycare
Centreville, MS

A Better Nametag

Clip-on nametags are durable, no-fuss alternatives to the ordinary variety. Prepare nametags as desired and laminate. Then glue a clothespin to the back of each nametag. For storing the nametags, secure both ends of a length of wide ribbon to a wall at students' eye level. Clip the nametags to the ribbon. As he enters the classroom, each student locates his tag and clips it to his clothing. These convenient clip-on tags are a snap for youngsters to use.

Sheryl Nash
Liverpool, NY

Wallpaper Nametags

Try this alternative to construction paper nametags. Cut sheets of wallpaper into 8½" x 11" rectangles so that they fit into your copy machine. Choose a favorite nametag pattern and duplicate it onto the wallpaper. Cut out the shapes. Then use an over-sized safety pin to attach each personalized nametag to its owner's clothing. For added fun, look for wall-paper with thematic designs that correspond to your field trips or special events.

Jackie Wright—Preschool
Summerhill Children's House
Enid, OK

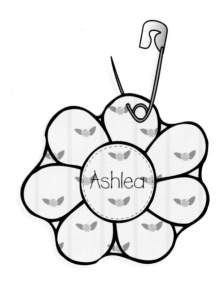

Nametags

Cubby Labels

Little ones will be able to easily locate their cubbies with these decorative labels. For each child, cut out a seasonal shape from poster board. Program each cutout with a different child's name; then mount his picture on his cutout. Laminate the cutouts if desired. Using Velcro fastener or tape, mount each cutout on a cubby. Your youngsters will be able to see at a glance where their cubbies are located.

Mary Borreca—Preschool/Special Needs
Martinsville Elementary
Martinsville, TX

The Name Escapes Me

Unless your substitute just happens to have a knack for recalling names, it's likely she'll appreciate this method. Write each child's name on a tagboard card. Then use a rectangle of clear self-adhesive covering to attach each name card to the back of the respective student's seat. As she's roaming the room supervising youngsters at work, it'll just take a glance at each nametag to give her the advantage of calling a youngster by name.

Brenda Purvis
Asheville Christian Academy
Asheville, N.C.

Nifty, Thrifty Nametags

Here's an idea for making nametags that are inexpensive and durable. Cut a classroom supply of shapes from light-colored felt. Use a permanent marker to label each shape with a different child's name. Spread a layer of glue across the back of the shape; then lay one side of a spring-type clothespin on the shape so that the gripping end is at the top of the nametag. When the glue is dry, these clip-on nametags are ready for action. So clip this idea to your must-do list!

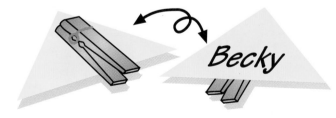

Becky Jones—Three- and Four-Year-Olds
Mt. Calvary Christian Preschool
Greenville, MI

Seasonal Seating

Here's a less permanent, yet long-lasting option for creating a seating arrangement in your group area. Each season or month, write a child's name on a decorative note-pad sheet. Tape the sheets to your group-area floor or carpet with several strips of clear, carton-sealing tape. You can vacuum, mop, or sweep over the shapes. What's more, when it's time for a change, the tape won't leave a sticky residue.

Sue DeMoss—Preschool, Maquoketa Head Start
Maquoketa, IA

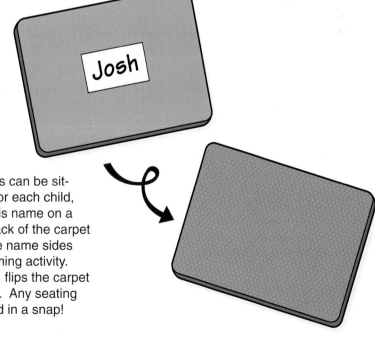

Carpet Capers

In just a few seconds your youngsters can be sitting pretty right where you want them. For each child, personalize a carpet square by writing his name on a sticky nametag and attaching it to the back of the carpet square. Arrange carpet squares, with the name sides up, in the style best suited to your upcoming activity. Then a youngster simply finds his name, flips the carpet over, and is seated on his carpet square. Any seating arrangement you desire can be achieved in a snap!

Denise Covert—Preschool
Shepherd of the Valley
Moreno Valley, CA

Seating

That Decorative Touch

Here's a tip that lends a creative flair to plain classroom carpets and/or individual student mats. (If you don't already have plain carpets or mats, check out carpet-store remnants or discount-store specials.) Gather a supply of stencils. Then use fabric paints to stencil around your carpet and mats.

And if you're into stenciling, invest a few more minutes in creating a special Share Chair that helps promote self-esteem, oral language, and vocabulary—not to mention a rhyme! Stencil the back and seat of a canvas director's chair. Invite children to sit in the chair for special times of sharing.

Ronda Caster, Supply Elementary, Supply, NC

Carpet Seating Assignments

Use carpet samples (purchased or donated from a carpet store) to create a large area rug for floor activities. To assemble an area rug, place identically sized carpet pieces facedown so that there are five rows of five pieces. Connect the pieces by taping the seams together using duct tape. Turn the area rug over. Then design a seating arrangement for typical floor activities by assigning each child her own carpet piece. For other types of activities, the patchwork layout of the rug can be used to space youngsters as necessary. For example, have students sit within the first two rows of carpet pieces during storytime or within the last two rows for viewing a video on an elevated TV screen. Your students will be snug as bugs on your new area rug!

Mary Johnson, Grandville Christian School, Grandville, MI

Have a Seat on a Shape

Use this management tip to provide each child with his own seat on the carpet, and review shapes and colors at the same time! Using geometric-shaped stencils and colorful paint, paint a variety of shapes in different colors onto your group-area carpet. When it's group time, invite each of your little ones to sit on a shape. Request, for example, that a child sit on a green shape or sit on a shape that is round. Not only are these shapes permanent, but they also add an attractive touch to your group space. Welcome to the group. Won't you please have a seat on a shape?

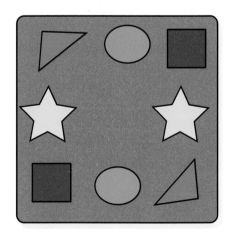

Lorna Friese—Three-Year-Olds
St. Mark's Nurturing Center
St. Charles, IL

Scissors Storage Can

If you want a practical and safe way to store scissors, this idea may be just what you need. For each table of students, turn a large empty can upside down. In the bottom of the can, drill a quantity of holes that are big enough for the pointed ends of students' scissors to fit through. Insert scissors in the holes, and put a can on each table. Since the scissors are in central locations, youngsters can get right to work.

Cindy Linton
Tuppers Plains Elementary School
Vincent, OH

Sentence Strip Space Saver

This idea will end your long search for a place to store sentence strips. The next time you or an acquaintance receives long-stemmed roses, save the box for storing sentence strips. (A local florist may be willing to donate boxes to your school.) Plainly label the boxes so you can determine their contents at a glance. Now that's the long and short of it!

Betty M. Jay
W.E. Cundiff Elementary
Vinton, VA

Colorful Crayon Holders

Reinforce visual-discrimination skills and also organize crayons with these neat crayon holders. Collect eight half-pint milk cartons for each table or station. Use construction paper to cover each milk carton in one set with one of the eight basic colors. Staple these eight cartons together to make one crayon holder. Repeat the process to assemble the remaining holders. Using self-adhesive labels, label the outside of each carton with its color's name. Sort a supply of crayons into each holder. Place a crayon holder on each table.

Alana Holley
Windmill Point Elementary
Port St. Lucie, FL

Storage

Ultra "Fab-ulous"

This idea not only helps clean up your classroom but models a great recycling concept to help clean up our earth as well. Have students bring in empty smaller-size detergent boxes. Cover the boxes with a colorful Con-Tact covering and use them for a variety of storage purposes such as storing math manipulatives, small game pieces, art supplies, file folders, crayons, and markers. The possiblilities are endless!

Debbie Buckley
Broadmoor Elementary
Lafayette, LA

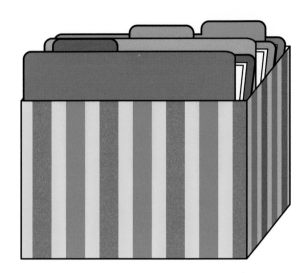

Expandable Files

Storing small classroom materials will be a breeze when using this helpful hint. Purchase expandable file folders tabbed with letters of the alphabet. Use one folder for storing laminated bulletin board letters and another folder for storing flannelboard pieces or even cookie cutters and play dough cutters.

Cindi Zsittnik
Wesley Grove PreK
Hanover, MD

Coffee Tin Organizers

All of those hard-to-keep-track-of school supplies can be right where you want them with this creative reuse of small flavored-coffee tins and lids. Place empty coffee tins in your desk drawer. In each tin, store a different item such as paper clips, thumbtacks, rubber bands, chalk, safety pins, and brads. Seal each tin with a lid labeled with that tin's contents. Celebrate the moments that you'll save looking for supplies!

Debra S. Bott
Duson Elementary
Scott, LA

Flannelboard Story Storage

Keep flannelboard stories and pieces accessible with this nifty storage idea. Insert each story into a clear, top-loading sheet protector. Put the accompanying pieces in the protector with the story. Then place all of the sheet protectors in a three-ring binder. Organize the binder seasonally or thematically to suit your needs.

Mary Anne Liptak—Four- and Five-Year-Olds
Lollipop Co-operative Preschool
Macedonia, OH

Baby Wipes Containers

If you want a practical way to store small classroom supplies, this idea may be just what you need. In advance, collect a quantity of empty baby wipes containers. Use them to store classroom supplies such as pencils, crayons, markers, and scissors, putting each in a different container. Label the outside of each container with the name of its contents and a picture of the contents. These nifty containers stack nicely and are easy for little hands to utilize.

Doris Peiffer
St. John's Christian Day Care
Monticello, IA

Banded Boxes

Keeping the lids on individual crayon boxes is a snap with this easy idea. Punch a hole in the center of a crayon box's lid. Slide a paper clip onto a rubber band. From the underside of the lid, thread the rubber band through the hole and pull it until the paper clip is flat against the lid. Secure the paper clip with a wide piece of tape. Place the lid on the box; then wrap the rubber band around the bottom of the box. Now crayons stay securely in their boxes and are easy to store.

Bernadette Hoyer—PreK
Howard B. Brunner School
Scotch Plains, NJ

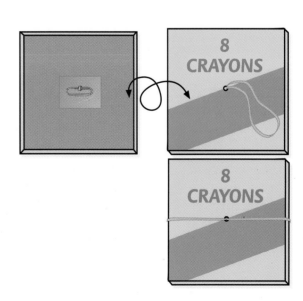

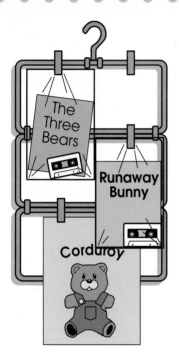

Book-and-Tape Holder

Hung up on how to store big books or book-and-tape sets? Try using a skirt hanger with multiple clips. Youngsters can identify, remove, and replace books with ease. Since most of these hangers will hold six books, you will want to change the book sets as your themes or seasons change.

Debbie Jones—Pre/K
Lorton, VA

Big-Book Storage

Make handy storage containers for your big-book collection by reusing the boxes that big books are shipped in. After saving a quantity of boxes, cut off one end of each. Use heavy, clear tape to reinforce each box. Then, with the opened end of each box facing up, hot glue the boxes together. Place two or three big books in each section for easy storage.

Jackie Wright—Gr. K and Preschool
Summerhill Children's House
Enid, OK

Perplexing Puzzle Pieces

Here's a way to keep your boxed puzzles organized and improve little ones' counting skills at the same time. Label each of your puzzle boxes with a different numeral; then label the back of the puzzle pieces in each set with the numeral on that puzzle's box. Encourage youngsters to store the puzzle boxes in numerical order when cleaning up. When a stray puzzle piece is found, simply match the numerals and it can quickly be returned to its box.

Carole Watkins—Program Coordinator
Holy Family Child Care Center
Crown Point, IN

Dishwasher Keepers

Here are some surprise uses for the dish racks and silverware holder from a discarded dishwasher. Stack books in dish racks with wheels for use as mobile book baskets. Mount the silverware basket to a wall (or set it in a center) for storage of crayons and markers. These handy items provide you with creative alternatives for organizing your classroom.

Deborah Kohanbash—Three-Year-Olds
Hillel School
Pittsburgh, PA

Rack 'em Up!

A colorful, plastic file crate makes the perfect puzzle rack for a preschool classroom. Simply turn the file crate on its side and slide the puzzles in! Little ones can put away puzzles quickly and easily with this attractive organizational method.

Debra Holbrook
Southern Baptist Educational Center
Olive Branch, MS

Puppet Window

If you have a three-piece folding puppet theater and not a lot of storage space, this idea is for you! Store the puppet theater in your dramatic play area behind the pretend sink. You will have more storage space and your little ones will have a window they can look out as they wash, wash, wash the dishes!

Storage

Big Book Storage

Rack up a classroom full of eager readers with a clothes-drying rack suspended from your classroom ceiling. Once the rack has been suspended at your youngsters' eye level, clip a big book or student-made book to each bar of the rack. When a student wants a book to read, the ones on this display are easy to find and accessible.

Ruth Fried
Clarks Summit, PA

Book/Cassette Sets

Keep books and cassettes together with zippered Press-on Pockets. Attach a small, Press-on Pocket inside the cover of a book and store the corresponding tape inside. Prepare two color-coded cutouts and attach one to the book and one to the cassette. Children will easily locate the sets they need.

Sheila Weinberg
Warren Point School
Fair Lawn, NJ

Book Displays

Hung up on how to store and display your collection of classroom books? Try using coat hangers. Mount screws or cup hooks on your wall; then place a hanger on each screw or hook. Open and drape multiple copies of a book over the bar of each hanger. Youngsters can identify, remove, and replace books with ease.

Sheri Dressler
Woodland School
Palatine, IL

Get Organized

It always pays to be organized. But if you organize and label your cupboards and drawers using bright-colored labels, volunteers and substitute teachers can see at a glance where to look for supplies. It's a timesaving method for everyone's benefit.

Linda Schwitzke—Preschool
Headstart
Longview, WA

Supply Trays

Little hands can get just what they need when you use these handy supply trays. In advance, collect a supply of various types of divided microwave meal trays. When you'd like to have small supplies within the reach of your little ones, use the trays that suit your needs. They're small enough to move from place to place and can be gathered up again in no time at all. If you use these trays for glue, the leftover glue can be peeled right off once it has dried. Simply supplied!

Beth Hall
Parkway Elementary School
Virginia Beach, VA

Hardware Storage Cabinets

End classroom clutter and store small items with this organizational idea. Purchase a hardware storage cabinet containing lots of drawers. Fill each drawer with a different type of small item such as paper clips, thumbtacks, staples, or rubber bands. Then label each drawer with its contents. For a variation, label each drawer with a different child's name. Fill each drawer with a different math manipulative such as craft sticks or small blocks. When it's time to use manipulatives, each child locates his name, removes his drawer from the storage cabinet, and is ready for math!

Juanita Pope
Eastside Elementary
Newnan, GA

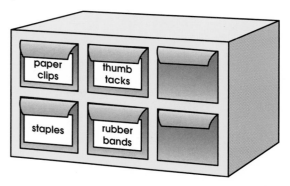

Storage

Picture Storage

Try this picture-perfect way to store your youngsters' photocopied photographs. In advance, purchase a hardware storage unit containing lots of miniature drawers. Photocopy a supply of each youngster's school photograph. Place each child's set of photos in a personalized drawer with his photo mounted on the outside of the drawer. When a student needs to use a photograph to personalize artwork or for graphing, he simply locates his drawer and takes out a picture.

Diane Harte
Swegles Elementary
St. John's, MI

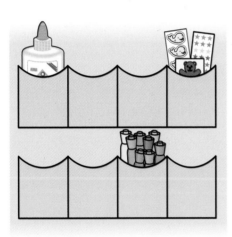

Storage Timesaver

If you often find yourself looking for supplies, save valuable teaching time by using a shoe bag to store items used most often. Hang the bag on the outside of your storage cabinet; then fill the pockets with frequently used items such as stickers, staplers, and glue. Be sure to store items for adult use—such as sharp scissors—out of your little ones' reach.

Melissa L. Epling—Preschool
Panther Creek Elementary
Nettie, WV

Catchall Containers

Ask families to help you collect the plastic containers from Lunchables prepared meals. Use these containers in your art center as individual trays for holding each child's paints, craft items, or collage materials. Or keep several containers near your desk for storing small objects such as pushpins or paper clips.

Christine Dise—Four-Year-Olds
Pottstown YMCA Childcare
Pottstown, PA

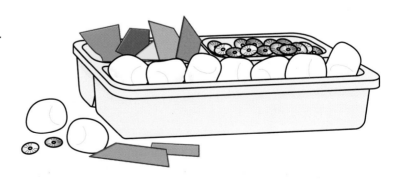

Colorful Crayon Holder

Reinforce visual discrimination and organize crayons with this neat crayon holder. Collect eight plastic cups, a cardboard food container that has eight sections (or two drink carriers with four sections each), and a wrapper from each of the eight different colors of jumbo crayons in a box. Tape a wrapper to each cup; then insert the cups in the sections of the container. Sort a supply of crayons into each cup. If desired tape the cover of a crayon box to a shelf to indicate where you would like the crayon holder to be stored when it's not in use.

Sue DeMoss
Maquoketa Head Start
Maquoketa, IA

Cool Storage

Are your shelves filled with worn-out and ripped boxes and scattered manipulatives? If so, try this cool idea for organizing them. Collect a supply of gallon-sized ice-cream buckets. Store small manipulatives—such as dominos, blocks, or milk jug lids—in each of the buckets. Label the outside front and back of each bucket with pictures of its contents. Not only will your shelves be organized, but youngsters will also know at a glance which bucket they want.

Patty Schmitt
St. Patrick's School
Portland, MI

Lovely Labels

When you use this easy tip for making picture labels for containers and shelves, children will know at a glance where everything belongs! Make a color or black-and-white photocopy of each item to be stored or shelved. Cut out the pictures; then use clear Con-Tact covering to attach them to the appropriate shelves or containers. During cleanup times, students can refer to the pictures in order to replace materials easily.

Mandi King—PreK
Hubbard PreK
Forsyth, GA

Storage

Keeping Track of Materials

As you clean and pack up materials at the end of this year, start preparing for your next school year by making these handy checklists. Use a separate open grid to list each group of materials—such as big books, flannelboard pieces, and manipulatives. Fill in the tops of the grids with the months that you are in school. Slide the grids between two construction-paper covers; then bind them together. As you write lesson plans the next school year, check off the month(s) that each material is used. Planning is much easier when you have a list of materials at your fingertips. No more rummaging through closets and cabinets!

Jackie Wright—Preschool
Summerhill Children's House
Enid, OK

Carryall Jugs

Use this idea for easy-to-carry manipulative storage. Collect a supply of large, empty, and clean laundry detergent jugs. Saw the top off each jug and file the rough edges with an emery board or cover them with masking tape. Cover the old label with white Con-Tact paper. Then use colorful permanent markers to label each jug and illustrate its new contents. These jugs are perfect for preschoolers because they are easy to carry, materials are visible, and cleanup is a snap!

Elesa Miller
St. Catherine Laboure School
Wheaton, MD

Add-On Hangers

Use add-on hangers to organize posters, charts, and small centers. Clip the materials to the hangers using both sides and link the hangers together. Your materials are right at your fingertips and it proves to be a real space saver.

Pat Marr
Taft School
Ferndale, MI

Thematic Storage Boxes

Decorate your room and store your teaching materials at the same time. Here's how! Decorate boxes to reflect the thematic materials they will hold. For example, for a farm-related unit, cover a box and its lid with colorful paper. Then glue on farm animal die-cut shapes. Or, for a transportation unit, cover a box with yellow paper. Add black paper wheels, painted windows, and magazine cutout passengers. You'll be able to tell at a glance where your materials for each theme are located. Plus it's a great way to spark youngsters' curiosity for upcoming units!

Amy Aloi and Gwen Blake—Four-Year-Olds
Berkshire Elementary
Forestville, MD

Get Organized! Bag It!

Organize desk items using the wide variety of gift bags that are available. Each month place a different bag on your desk to store notepads, stickers, nametags, and awards. Use seasonal and holiday bags such as a bunny bag for Easter or a flower bag for spring. This is a fun and festive way to dress up your desk and to end clutter.

Susan M. Nutzman
North Elementary School
Falls City, NE

Storage

Supply List

Keeping track of the supplies you need will be an easy task with this organizational tip. Write a list of your classroom supplies on a sheet of paper and make multiple copies. Keep a copy of the list on the inside of a cupboard door and anywhere else supplies are stored. Whenever you run out of a particular item, mark the item on the list. On your next shopping trip, take the lists with you; then replace each list with a new one.

Mary E. Maurer—Preschool
Children's Corner
Durant, OK

Teacher's Tool Belt

Try this idea when you need supplies right at your fingertips. Purchase a muslin tool belt from a hardware store. Sponge-paint or stencil the pockets of the tool belt with the designs of your choice. Place frequently used items such as stickers, pens, markers, glue, and scissors in the pockets of the tool belt. Since supplies are right at hand when you are sporting your teacher's tool belt, valuable time is saved.

Nancy Smith
Capac Elementary
Washington, MI

Clay Pot Organizer

Get organized and end desk clutter with this tidy tip. Purchase a clay pot (found in nurseries and plant stores) for storing stickers, pencils, scissors, and notepads. To decorate your pot, spray paint it white and allow it to dry. Then paint the pot with a picture or design of your choice. Fill the pot with the small items that usually clutter your desktop. Place the pot of supplies on your desk, and your desktop will not only be more organized; it will be more attractive too.

Mona Coker Smith
Collinsville Elementary
Collinsville, AL

Puppets on a String

Need a clever way to store puppets? Here's a space-saving idea you can really hang on to! Hang a plastic chain with clips (available at discount stores) from your classroom ceiling. Clip the puppets available for student use on the part of the chain that is within youngsters' reach. Hang the remaining puppets higher on the chain.

Laura Sacco—Four-Year-Olds
East Woods School
Oyster Bay, NY

Puppet Holder

Keep your puppets organized with this convenient storage idea. Purchase a pocket shoe organizer and mount it at students' eye level on your wall or closet door. Store a different puppet in each pocket. Both you and your little ones will have easy access to puppets using this neat and handy tip.

Linda Anne Lopienski, Asheboro, NC

Puppet Posts

Organize your puppets with these easy-to-make puppet posts! First, obtain a sturdy, medium-size box with a lid and six to eight paper towel tubes. Trace one end of each tube onto the lid. Use a utility knife to cut out the resulting circles. Insert the tubes into the holes, securing them with hot glue. Pack the tubes with newspaper; then seal the ends with packing tape. Finally, spray-paint the box and the tubes. When the paint is dry, place your puppets on the posts. There you have it—perfectly pleasing puppet storage!

Leigh A. Allen—Two-, Three-, and Four-Year-Olds
Virginia Commonwealth University Child Care Center
Richmond, VA

Storage

Puppet Holder

Conveniently display classroom puppets on a plastic, freestanding shoe rack. Slip each puppet over a plastic loop on the shoe rack. Your youngsters will have easy access to puppets when using this helpful hint.

Lois A. Waltz—PreK–K
St. Ambrose School
Old Bridge, NJ

Inventory Notebook

Do you find it difficult to keep track of the many resources you've accumulated for each of your thematic units? Try creating a notebook to keep an inventory of your materials. After dividing your resources into boxes labeled for each theme or topic, designate a notebook page for each box. On that page, list all the items in that particular box. When you're ready to start a new unit, pull out the notebook, locate the page designated for the theme or topic, and scan the page so you won't miss any useful resources.

Deborah Pruett—Preschool
St. Mary of the Woods College, Woods Preschool
St. Mary of the Woods, IN

Monthly Boxes

No more endless searching for ideas when you organize your classroom materials in monthly storage boxes. Collect a box with a lid for each month that you teach. Label the outside of each box with a different month; then store your seasonal books, games, decorations, and centers inside the appropriate box. List the contents of each box on a piece of tagboard; then glue the tagboard onto the side of the box. Now all of your seasonal materials will be right at your fingertips.

Elaine Galeazzi
Trabert Center
Knoxville, IA

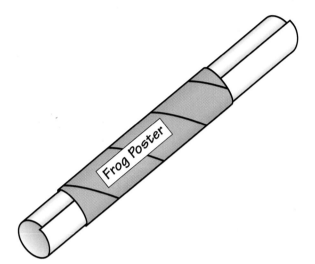

Theme Chart Storage

Save wrapping paper and paper towel tubes for storing charts and posters that go with your themes. Roll up a chart or poster, and place it inside a tube. Label the outside of the tube with the theme title and store the tube in the corresponding theme box. Classroom charts and posters will be easily accessible and well protected.

Faith Shiver
Lillian E. Williams Elementary School
Attapulgus, GA

Weekly Organization

Organize the teaching materials that you'll need for the week with this idea. Label each of five large wicker baskets with a different day of the week. Sort your teaching materials—such as books, poems, flannelboard pieces, cassette tapes, puppets, and games—for each day into the appropriate basket. With this system, daily planning will be simplified and materials will be easy to locate.

B. Childery—Three-, Four-, and Five-Year-Olds
Walnut Creek Elementary
Azle, TX

Boo-Boo Basket

Next time your little ones get a boo-boo, come to the rescue with this handy first aid kit. To prepare a kit, fill a picnic-type basket with supplies, such as cartoon-printed adhesive bandages, rubber gloves, diaper wipes, facial tissues, cotton balls, and stickers. If desired, use child-friendly names to refer to each item, such as "magic tear-catchers" for tissues. Each time you head outdoors for recess or a field trip, just grab the basket and go.

Shari Caruthers—Four-Year-Olds
Presbyterian Day School
Memphis, TN

Storage

Pizza Plus!

What's better than a hot, fresh-from-the-oven pizza? The box it comes in! Pizza boxes hold lots of materials, are easy to label, and stack well for storage. Wipe the inside of a used box with a damp cloth. If desired, cover and line the box with Con-Tact covering. Need extras? Here's a good excuse to order more pizza! (Or politely ask your neighborhood pizza parlor for donations.) A great idea any way you slice it!

Doris Porter—Preschool
Headstart
Anamosa, IA

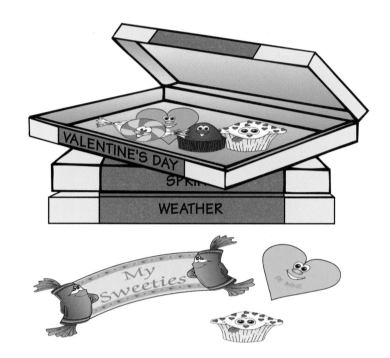

Box It Up

Store small items—such as bulletin board letters, stickers, and small manipulatives—in plastic videocassette boxes. Label each box with its contents; then store the boxes on a shelf or in a cupboard.

Amy Drake—Two-Year-Olds
Westview Childcare Ministry
Fort Wayne, IN

Decorative Carriers

It's easy to tell that school papers are special when they come home tucked in beautifully decorated tubes. Have students decorate cardboard tubes using an assortment of art supplies. Label each child's tube with his name or have him label it. When artwork or notices need to go home, roll each student's papers and tuck them into his tube for transport.

A Special Space

Foster a sense of classroom ownership and belonging by inviting each child to create his own special space in your classroom. A couple of weeks before school starts, mail each child a notecard inviting him (and his parent) to drop by your classroom on a designated date. (Use your open house date if your school holds one before classes start.) In the note, ask the child to bring requested school supplies with him on that day. When the child arrives, show him his cubby and where any larger supplies of his will be kept. Then give him a strip of tagboard labeled with his name. Encourage him to use an assortment of simple art supplies, such as stickers and stamps, to decorate his name-tag. Then help him post his nametag on his cubby or at a table space. Youngsters will rest easy knowing they have a special space in their new kindergarten classroom. And you'll rest easy knowing all those sets of school supplies are organized before that hectic first day of school!

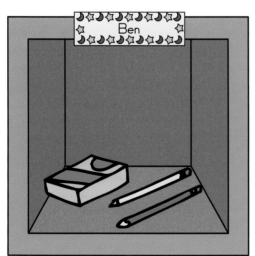

adapted from an idea by Kiva English
Cato-Meridian Central School
Elbridge, NY

You've Got Mail

This first-class way to create classroom mailboxes gets our stamp of approval. Obtain enough sturdy, compartmentalized boxes (such as those available at liquor stores) so that you have a separate compartment for each child, your assistant, and yourself. Tape the boxes together with duct tape; then cover the entire unit with decorative Con-Tact covering. Label each compartment with a different child's name and a reduced photocopy or color copy of his photo.

Put the mailboxes in a language center so that students can send each other messages and pictures. Or use the mailboxes as a handy way to communicate with parents. Have you checked your box lately? You've got mail!

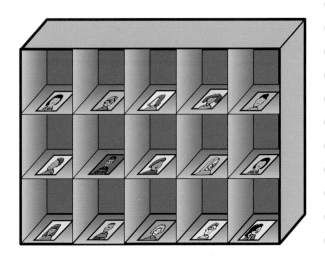

Elizabeth A. Cooper—PreK
Meadowbrook Elementary School
Fort Worth, TX

Keep the Change

If your youngsters sometimes lose their lunch or snack money, then try this efficient way to store it. In advance, purchase a hardware storage unit containing lots of miniature drawers. Personalize the outside of each drawer with a different student's name. Each morning as students enter the room, have each child place his lunch and/or snack money in his drawer. No more lost coins!

Brenda Wells and Donna Cook, Roseland Park Elementary, Picayune, MS

Clothespin Clippers

Here's a simple solution for keeping students' completed papers together until it's time to go home. Write each student's name on a different clothespin. Throughout the day, encourage each youngster to put each of his completed papers in his clothespin clip. At the end of the school day, have each student transport his papers and projects to his bookbag with the clothespin still attached. This method helps each student keep his papers together and eliminates the need for writing his name on wet artwork.

Kathleen A. Mullane
Middleport Elementary
Middleport, NY

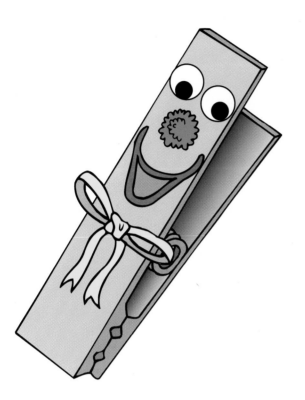

Hang It!

Use these nifty clothespins to hang and organize students' work and school papers. To make a character clothespin, glue wiggle eyes on a spring-type clothespin. Then glue on a small pom-pom for a nose and use puffy paint to make the mouth. Next, tie a bow from a narrow length of ribbon; then glue it under the mouth. Use a marker to write a child's name on the back of the clothespin. Clip a classroom supply of character clothespins to a suspended clothesline. Each day clip each student's work or school papers to his clothespin. At the end of the week, staple each child's papers together, and they are ready to go home.

Cymthan Sheikh—Preschool/Head Start
Ringgold Middle School
Ringgold, GA

Clip It!

Use clipboards to organize students' work and school papers. For each child, provide a clipboard that has a hole for hanging it up. Mount hanging hooks in a Peg-a-Board; then label each place with a child's name. When students arrive in the morning, request that they hang their clipboards on the hooks. Throughout the day, teachers and students can clip papers onto the clipboards as needed. At the end of the day, packing up is quick and easy because each child's papers are all in one place. Parents can also use the clipboard to send papers or messages back to you. It's easy—just clip it!

Martha Ann Davis
Pinecrest Elementary
Greenwood, SC

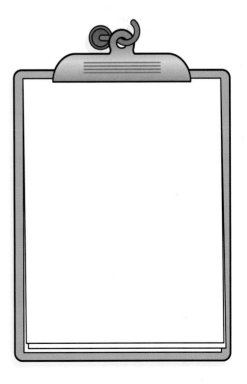

Storage

Where's My Pencil?

Do your youngsters often lose or mispace their pencils? Eliminate this problem with self-adhesive Velcro tape. Cut a length of Velcro tape long enough to wrap around a pencil. Peel the paper off the back of the Velcro pieces. Wrap the loop side around the top of each child's pencil and mount the hook side inside his desk or on his tabletop. When a child is not using his pencil, he simply attaches the pencil to his desk or tabletop. This simple technique is sure to keep pencils right at your youngsters' fingertips.

Shari O'Shea
Conewago Elementary School
Elizabethtown, PA

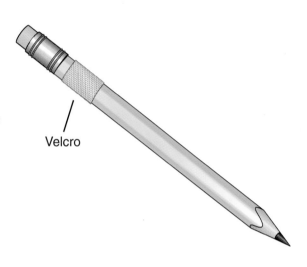

Velcro

Hooked on It!

Coat hooks mounted too high or too sparsely can be chaos in a kindergarten classroom! Solve the problem with cuphooks. Screw one cup hook in the underside of a coat closet shelf for each extra hook needed. From each cup hook, hang a personalized closet organizer as shown. Getting everything within your little ones' reach will help promote independence and responsiblility as well as a more pleasant classroom environment.

Gayle Young
Evans Elementary School
Evans, GA

Curriculum Ties and Lesson Helps

Contents

Assessment

Personal Portfolios

Enlist the help of children's families to decorate portfolio boxes for storage of students' work throughout the year. Collect a class supply of empty cereal boxes. Cut the top flaps off the boxes; then cover each box with paper. Personalize each box before sending it home along with a note suggesting that a parent help his child decorate the box. Hang the returned boxes on a clothesline in your room. When you want to save an item for a child's portfolio of work, simply slip the item into his box. What a decorative way to store your little ones' work!

Kim Spankowski—Four-Year-Olds
Kenosha Unified School District Head Start
Kenosha, WI

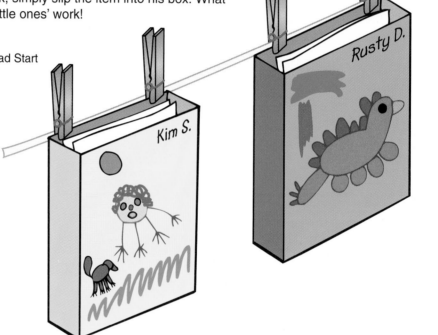

Lists, Lists, Lists!

Here is an easy way to keep track of your students' progress. Make a list of class names on a 4" x 5" sheet of paper, and draw a line after each name. Make multiple copies of this list to be used for various tasks. Use these lists to check off children as they rotate through different learning centers, visit the library, or are evaluated on various skills. Keep a list next to your door so you have easy access to it during a fire drill or school trip.

Wilma Droegemueller—PreK and K
Zion Lutheran School
Mt. Pulaski, IL

Brett ___✓___
Cary ___✓___
Cheryl _____
Christopher _____
David _____
Dianne_____
Gage ___✓___
Gail_____
Jordan ___✓___
Jaden_____
Rebecca _____
Ryan ___✓___
Zachary ___✓___

Seasonal Assessment

If you like to keep a record of students' language development, try this idea to speed up interviewing and make students' answers attractive for display and easy to file. First, type the question you will ask all of your students. For each child, print the question on a label sticker. Stick the label on a piece of shaped notepaper; then record the child's answer to the question on the paper. Display the responses for parents to enjoy. Later, file the notes in students' individual folders. Try this method after you complete thematic units or after special events such as field trips.

Valerie Corbeille—Four-Year-Olds
New Life Christian Preschool
Maple Valley, WA

Notable Records

Make a note of student progress as soon as you observe it. Keep a pocketful of Post-It notes. (If you have a small class, using a different color for each child can be helpful.) To record an observation, write it on a note, date it, and attach it to a blank chart. File the notes in individual student records at a more convenient time.

Cathie Pesa—Special Needs Preschool
Youngstown City Schools
Boardman, OH

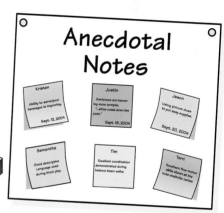

Handy Information Cards

Here's an idea that will keep student information at your fingertips. On a 3" x 5" index card for each youngster, list important information such as the student's name, address, phone number, birthday, parents' names, and emergency information. Punch a hole in the upper right-hand corner of each card; then put all of the cards on a large metal ring. Fasten the ring onto a drawer handle for easy access or onto your purse strap for field trips. These cards also come in handy when checking students' personal information skills.

Debbie Peters
Avondale Elementary
Marion, AR

Assessment

Anecdotal Recording

Keep track of anecdotal comments with this quick recording system. Draw lines inside a file folder to visually divide it into approximately three-inch squares. Label each box with a child's name. During the day, record anecdotal notes on small self-sticking notes, and attach each note to the appropriate child's box. At the end of the day or week, you can quickly transfer the notes to each child's individual records. This system will provide you with a variety of specific notes for your own reference and parent conferences.

Linda Crosby
Hill Crest Community School
Fort Vermilion, Alberta, Canada

Mary shared toys April 10	John	Eva	Tim follows directions April 10	Bryan
Martin	Alex	Jackson listens to others April 1	Ben	Samuel
Maggie	Beth	Jimah talks to everyone April 10	Mai sings loudly and smiles April 9	Tanisha
Erica	Angel	Scotty	Jacob	Jeremy

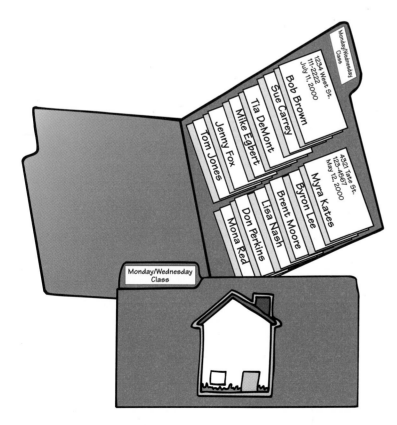

Class Information Folder

Have students' personal information right at your fingertips when you organize it in a folder. For each child, program the front of an index card with his name, address, phone number, and birthday. Program the back of each child's card with other important information, such as the names of the adults who are permitted to pick him up from school. Alphabetize the cards. Then tape them to the inside of the folder, staggering them as shown. If desired, tape additional index cards under each child's information card to use for anecdotal records. This system is a great way to keep all of your important student information in one place.

Penni Wells—PreK
Park Village Elementary
San Antonio, TX

Organizing Individual Centers

Need to organize your individual centers? If so, try this management aid. Store the pieces of individual centers—such as lotto, tangrams, or cards—in different gallon-size resealable plastic bags. Label the outside of each bag with its contents. Place four or five bags in a cardboard magazine holder. Then arrange the magazine holders on a table so youngsters have easy access to the centers.

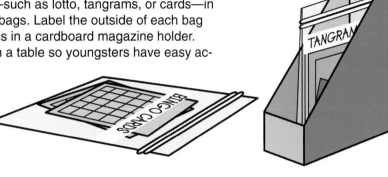

Sue Elliott
Ruskin Elementary School
Ruskin, FL

Playing Places

These tablecloth play stations help define children's play spaces, and they speed up cleanup too! To get started, arrange a few vinyl, flannel-backed tablecloths on the floor. Then place a different tub of toys or manipulatives on each tablecloth. Assign a different group of children to each tablecloth. Ask each group to play or work on its assigned tablecloth. When it's time to clean up, your little ones know where the little things go!

Joyce Cummings—PreK
First Baptist Day School
O'Fallon, MO

Quick Identification

Use small wooden cutouts from craft stores to help your little ones identify their cubbies, coat hooks, and learning centers. For each child, purchase multiple copies of a different wooden cutout. If the cutouts are unpainted, identically paint each set of matching cutouts. Have each child select a cutout design; then hot-glue the matching cutouts onto his cubby and coat hook.

Use the remaining cutouts to manage the flow of students in learning centers. To the back of each of the cutouts, attach the loop side of a Velcro circle. Attach the hook sides of the Velcro circles to learning center signs. When a student selects a center to visit, he attaches his cutout to the corresponding sign.

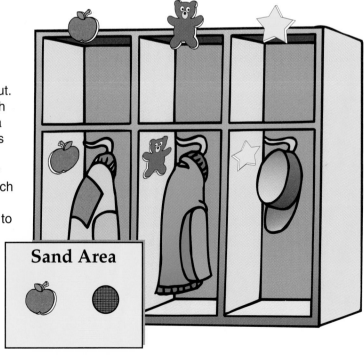

Sand Area

Amy Aloi—Three- and Four-Year-Olds
Prince Georges County Head Start
Bladensburg, MD

Centers

Colored Clothespins

Since clothespins are often used for a variety of matching games and centers, this tip might be just what you need to keep them organized. Dye a quantity of wooden clothespins by mixing one package of fabric dye and hot water in an old pan. Place the clothespins in the dye for a few minutes; then rinse them with cold water. Using different colors of dye, tint additional clothespins. Use each color of clothespins with a different center. If a clothespin gets separated from its center, you can see at a glance where it belongs!

Carol J. McClintick
Sanford Elementary School
Midland, MI

A Tidy Tip

Use this suggestion and your classroom could be practically spotless! Place a container of disposable pop-up wipes in your arts-and-crafts center. Encourage your students to use a wipe whenever one is needed. This tidy tip can put an end to paint stains, messy glue bottles, and especially grimy little hands.

Pat Bollinger
Leopold R-3
Leopold, MO

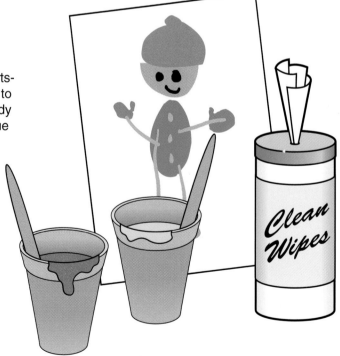

Snappy Center Management

Youngsters will independently choose and change learning centers with this photographic management system. Take an individual photo of each child and each of your classroom centers. Mount each picture onto a same-size piece of cardboard. Cover each mounted photo with clear Con-Tact covering; then attach a piece of magnetic tape to the back of it. Use masking tape to visually divide a magnetic surface into a grid with enough spaces for each center's photo and the number of children you will allow in that center at one time. Arrange the pictures of the centers on the grid. When choosing a center, a child places her picture in a space next to her chosen center's photo. When all the spaces are filled, the center is full.

Christine Zieleniewski—PreK
Saint Cecilia School
Kearny, NJ

Center Signs

Create colorful signs to help your youngsters remember how many children are allowed at each of your centers. For each center, label a sheet of colored construction paper with the center name. Then cut a number of shape cutouts (such as stars or hearts) from a complementary color of construction paper. Determine the number of students you wish to visit a particular center. Glue the corresponding number of shape cutouts to that center's sign. Laminate all the signs and post them near your centers. Students can tell at a glance how many children are allowed and can count heads to figure out if there is room for one more!

Tracy Tavernese—Four-Year-Olds
Holy Child School
Old Westbury, NY

Centers

Center Signs and Markers

These signs and markers will help organize your center time. Create a center marker for each child by painting either a person or bunny on a flat clothespin. Label each child's clothespin with her name; then affix a strip of magnetic tape to the back. Keep all the clothespins on a magnet board in your classroom.

To make a sign for each center, spray-paint a brick and a wooden dowel. Glue a piece of felt to the bottom of the brick to prevent it from scratching the floor. Insert the dowel into the center hole of the brick. Screw a cup hook into the top of the dowel. Label a 10" x 12" piece of tagboard with a numeral to indicate how many children may play at that center. Outline a corresponding number of flat clothespins, to match the design of your center markers, below the numeral. Laminate the sign; then affix a strip of magnetic tape within the outline of each clothespin. (Be sure to place the magnetic tape pieces so they will attract the magnetic tape on the clothespins.) Punch a hole in the top of each sign and hang it from the cup hook at that center.

When it's time for centers, have each child find her marker and attach it to the sign at the center where she wishes to play.

Chris Garchow—PreK, St. Paul's Lutheran School, Janesville, WI

Center Punch Card

To ensure your youngsters' participation in each classroom center, try this technique. Label each of your centers with a shape cutout—having no two identical shapes the same color. For each child, program and color a construction paper strip with the corresponding shapes. During center time, have each student carry his strip from station to station. When he has completed a center, punch the matching shape on his strip and have him select his next station. Encourage students to visit each of the centers represented on their strips and have their strips punched accordingly. It's easy to see at a glance which centers a student still needs to visit.

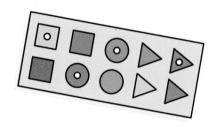

Barbara Pasley—Special Education, Energy Elementary, Energy, IL

Flag Time

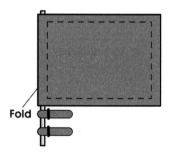

Fly a different color of flag at each of your centers to help children choose and change areas with ease. To make a flag, fold a long, rectangular piece of felt in half and stitch around all four sides, stitching about ½-inch from the fold on the folded side. (This will create a casing along the folded side.) Insert a wooden dowel in the casing, and hot-glue the flag in place if necessary. To make a flag stand, drill a hole in a block of wood and insert the flagpole. Place a flag at each center. Attach colored clothespins to each flagpole according to the number of children who may be in that center. When a child enters a center, he takes a clothespin from the flagpole and clips it to his clothing. When he leaves that center, he replaces the clothespin on the flagpole.

Carla J. Moore, Washington District Elementary School, Buckhannon, WV

Next Stop!

This center-management idea is just the ticket for promoting decision-making skills! In turn, ask each child to name his center choice; then give him a train ticket to that center. Invite one student to be the engineer. Ask the other students to "get on board" (line up) behind him. Instruct the engineer to lead the student train around the room, stopping at each center. When the train arrives at a center, have him announce the stop and take the tickets of students who are disembarking to play at that station. Next stop, sand table! Toot, toot!

Margaret Mankiewicz—Special Needs/Preschool
Vineyard's Elementary School
Naples, FL

Flannelboard Choices

To make choosing centers a simple matter, set up this color-coded management system. Display a different-colored tagboard square in each of your centers; then cut a smaller square from each different color of tagboard. Back each smaller square with felt for use on the flannelboard. Label each square with the corresponding center's name; then draw a picture to represent that center. Personalize a felt square for each child. To use this system, arrange the labeled squares across the top of a flannelboard. Give each child his personalized square to place on the flannelboard under the square that represents the center of his choice.

Tracy Farrell—PreK
St. Columba School
St. Paul, MN

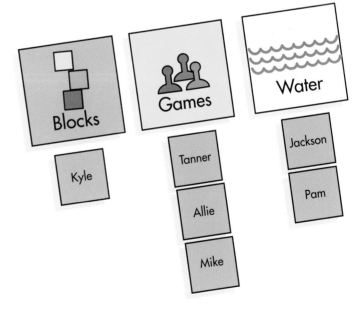

Centers

Learning Centers Chart

Create a learning centers chart in a snap with this picture-perfect idea. To make a chart, take a picture of each learning center sign in your room. Next, take a picture of each child in your class. After the pictures have been developed, mount the center pictures onto one side of a large piece of oaktag. Laminate the pictures of the children; then cut them out. Place a small ball of Sticky-Tac on the back of each child's picture. Attach the pictures near the center photos to indicate which centers the students are to visit. Or have a child find his picture and attach it to the chart beside the center picture of his choice.

Joan Johnson—PreK
Columbus School
Bridgeport, CT

Portable Centers

Short on center space? Here's a practical tip. Make your writing and art centers portable by using fast-food drink carriers and 16-ounce plastic cups. Label a sentence strip with the center's name; then attach the strip to the side of the carrier. Insert a cup into each of the carrier's sections. Fill each cup with a different item, such as markers, glue, or scissors. Set the tray on a table and voilà, an instant center!

adapted from an idea by JoAnn Brukiewa—PreK
St. Clare School
Baltimore, MD

Here's the Ticket

Looking for a way to organize your learning center time? If so, then this idea may be just the ticket you need! Request that a home supply store donate countertop samples that are no longer in use. To make a ticket for each child, trim his picture; then tape it onto a sample. Personalize the tickets. In each of your classroom centers, screw as many cup hooks into a wooden surface as you will allow children in that center at one time. Store the tickets near your group area. To choose a center, a child hangs his ticket on one of the center's hooks.

Nicky Daigle—Non-Categorical Preschool
Thibodaux Elementary
Thibodaux, LA

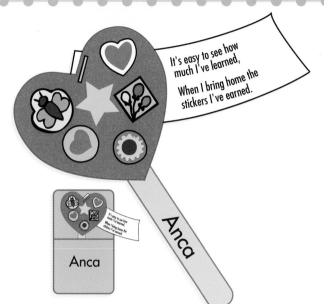

It's easy to see how much I've learned, When I bring home the stickers I've earned.

Anca

"Pop-Sticker" Collections

Encourage your little ones to complete learning centers by rewarding them with monthly sticker collections. Personalize a library pocket for each child; then mount the pockets to a piece of poster board. Each month, glue a seasonal shape to an ice-cream stick for each child. Personalize the sticks; then place each child's stick in his pocket on the chart. When a child completes a learning center, attach a sticker to his shape. At the end of each month, send the "pop-sticker" collections home with notes similar to the one shown.

Gloria Whitley—Preschool, G.U.M. Preschool, Mesa, AZ

Puzzle Problem Solver

Do lost puzzle pieces have you puzzled? If so, then here's a tip for you. On newspaper, have youngsters assemble each of your puzzles to be sure that you have all of the pieces. Then flip each puzzle over so that it is facedown. Spray-paint the puzzles' bottoms using a different color for each puzzle. After the paint dries, place the puzzles back in your puzzle center and use the puzzles as before. This easy color-coding method will help youngsters see at a glance which puzzle pieces belong together.

Maria Cuellar Munson
Unity Church Preschool
Garland, TX

Center Rotation

To establish groups and ensure that youngsters rotate through all of your structured learning centers, try this technique. Label each of the centers in your rotation with a different-colored bird cutout. Prepare a matching set of bird cutouts for each center so that the total number of cutouts equals the number of students in your class. Laminate the cutouts and then glue each one to a clothespin. When the glue is dry, store the resulting clips in a container. When it's center time, ask each child to close his eyes and choose a clip to wear. Group the children by the color of their clips and send them to the corresponding centers. During the remainder of your center time, rotate the groups until each group has visited each center.

adapted from an idea by Sandy DiFilippo—Four-Year-Olds
Laurel Park & Recreation Preschool
Laurel, MD

Cookie Cutter Center Tags

If you're looking for a way to organize your learning center time, then this idea might be cut out just for you! In each center, nail as many picture-frame hooks into the wall—or attach as many self-adhesive hooks onto the wall—as you will allow children in that center at one time. Obtain a class supply of plastic cookie cutters that have hooks for hanging. Give each child a different-shaped cookie cutter. To choose a center, a child simply hangs his cutter on one of a center's hooks.

Dawn Hansen—Preschool
Lasting Impressions Preschool
Kankakee, IL

Clip-a-Center

Youngsters can independently choose and change learning centers with this colorful management system. To prepare, cut a different-colored tagboard square for each of your learning centers. Label each sign. Color the same number of clothespins to match a center's sign as you will allow children in that center at one time. Clip the clothespins to the appropriate signs; then place the signs in the centers. When visiting a center, a child removes a clothespin from that center's sign and clips it to his clothing. When no more clothespins are available on a sign, that center is full. When leaving a center, a child replaces the clothespin on the sign.

Susan Burbridge—Preschool
Trinity Methodist Weekday School
San Antonio, TX

Housekeeping

Play Dough Volunteers

Do you have parents who would love to help out but can't come to school during the day? Get them involved by asking them to make batches of play dough. At the beginning of the year, ask each interested parent to sign up for the month she is willing to make a batch of dough. Then distribute copies of the recipe. To give each parent a friendly reminder when it's her turn to make play dough, just give her a phone call or send home another copy of the recipe. This idea is sure to save you lots of time, and it will ensure that your children always have fresh dough for your play dough center.

Gerene Thom—Five-Year-Olds/Transitional Kindergarten
Denmark Early Childhood Center
Denmark, WI

Play Dough Volunteers		
Aug.	Gerene Thom	655-4331
Sept.	Susan Bowers	632-1174
Oct.	Mike Mann	605-7742

Play Dough Recipe

Tired of looking for a play dough recipe each time you need a new batch in your play dough center? If so, try this timesaving tip. Using a permanent marker, program a play dough container with your favorite play dough recipe. This will save you lots of time and will be easy for parents, substitutes, and fellow teachers to locate.

Angela Anderson—Preschool
Richland County Cooperative Preschool
Mansfield, OH

Board Game Leftovers

If you have board games with missing pieces, check those boxes before tossing them in the trash! Take out any dice, timers, spinners, card trays, or other useful items for future use in your classroom centers. These are especially helpful when you create your own games. Shop yard sales, too, to find board game treasures!

Diana Berrios—Three- and Four-Year-Olds
Bright Beginnings
Sewell, NJ

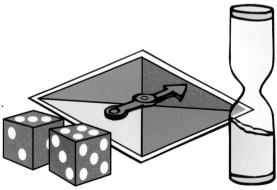

Centers

A Sticky Solution

Simplify your life with this easy way to cut out patterns from felt or fabric! Trace or draw the pattern on a piece of Con-Tact paper. Cut out the pattern, peel off the backing from the paper, and then stick the pattern onto the fabric. Next, using the pattern as a guide, cut the shape out of the fabric. Then peel off the pattern and use it again in the same manner. What a terrific way to make pieces for your flannelboard center!

Jeanine Trofholz—Three-Year-Olds
St. Luke's Rainbow Preschool
Columbus, NE

Durable Bookmarkers

Have you ever wondered how to get your students to return books to the proper places in your classroom reading center? Try using durable bookmarkers! Cut the covers from vinyl notebooks into wide strips. Then write a different child's name on each strip. As a child takes a book from the shelf, instruct him to insert his bookmarker in the book's place. When he returns the book to the shelf, he simply locates his bookmarker and replaces the book as he slides the bookmarker out of place.

Sheryl Spears, Idalia School, Wray, CO

Made in the Shade

A colorful beach umbrella can brighten any classroom. Purchase an inexpensive beach umbrella. (Watch for sales toward summer's end.) To anchor the umbrella, half-fill a sand pail with plaster of paris. Prop the umbrella in an upright position in the plaster until it dries. Later, fill the rest of the pail with sand and some shells. Finally, place the umbrella on a table in a learning center. Cool idea, dude!

Lesson Plan Helper

Save time writing lesson plans each week with this preprogrammed helper. Clip two acetate sheets on top of two blank pages in your lesson plan book. Using a permanent marker, program regular weekly activities such as lunch, naptime, and music. Remove the sheets and program your plan book with the week's special lessons and activities; then reattach the preprogrammed sheets. For faster weekly planning, you'll see that this method is clearly better!

Barbara Smith
Forest North Elementary
Austin, TX

9–9:30	Calendar
10:30	Snack
11–11:30	Music
12:00	Dismissal

Unit Record

Organize your teaching units with this handy tip. Complete a one-page unit record listing all of the materials that you have available for a particular unit, such as books, films, poems, games, and songs. Once your unit record is complete, use it to speed you along as you write your lesson plans. Reuse this record from year to year. It's a great way to jog your memory about the resources you have collected.

Mary Tamporello
Wyandotte Elementary
Morgan City, LA

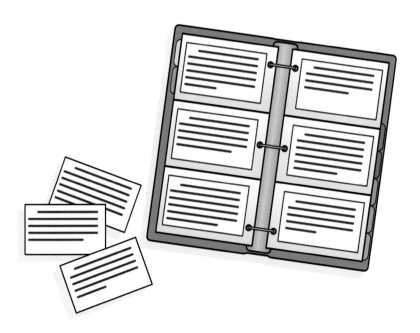

Photo Album Organization

No more endless searching for that cute idea that you remember seeing somewhere! Using colored index tabs, label sections of a photo album with categories such as Halloween, Christmas, spring, and animals. Print songs, fingerplays, games, or other ideas on index cards. Slide each card into a slot in the album. Then those ideas are readily available when you need them.

Beth Prawdzik—Pre/K
Somerset School
Troy, MI

Lesson Plans

Make the Most of *The Mailbox*®

The Mailbox will be right at your fingertips with this organized alternative. Cut two pieces of 6" x 7" tagboard, insert seven to ten pieces of 6" x 7" paper between the tagboard, and bind together in booklet form. On the cover, list the year and subjects contained in *The Mailbox*. Color code the subjects and make matching color tabs for the various sections of the book. Make a copy of the "Index to *The* Preschool *Mailbox*" (found in June/July issues), which summarizes the yearly units. Cut each subject apart and glue it to the appropriate section in the book. This will make a handy reference book!

Doris Wilcox
West Elementary
Levelland, TX

The Mailbox Keepsake

Try this organized filing system to centralize your favorite ideas from *The Mailbox*. Attach labeled tabs representing upcoming units to pages from a loose-leaf photo album. Put several pages behind each tab in the album. Clip or photocopy ideas from *The Mailbox* that you want to keep on file. Place the ideas in the appropriate section of the album. This handy reference will make finding ideas a snap.

Amy Pylant
Killarney Elementary
Orlando, FL

Three-Ring Binder

If your file folders are filled to the brim and you have difficulty locating ideas, then try this filing system. Keep ideas organized in a three-ring binder containing pocket dividers. Label each pocket with its contents, such as art ideas, fingerplays, games, or math activities. In each pocket, store corresponding ideas, lessons, and activities. Using this binder, you'll be able to locate what you need with ease!

Janet Koenig
Riverview Pre/K
Sioux City, IA

Literature Index

When gathering books for teaching your next unit, grab an index card too. Label the top of the card with your unit's theme. As you find related books, list their titles and their locations on the card. Store the cards for the units you teach together in an index card file box. This information will be a huge time-saver the next time you prepare to teach a favorite unit.

Robin Love Bowman—Preschool
St. Joseph Preschool
Owosso, MI

Easy Literature Reference

Make the most of *The Mailbox®* literature ideas and activities by using this organizational tip. Reproduce any literature activities or sections from the magazine; then glue or clip them to the back of your personal copy of the corresponding book. Label each book that contains an activity from *The Mailbox* by placing a blank adhesive dot or sticker on the spine. You'll be able to look at your classroom library and see at a glance which books have extension activities.

Robin Gattis
Seagoville Elementary School, Seagoville, TX

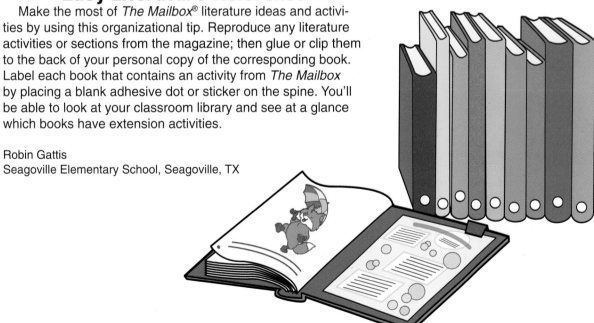

Book Bear

Students can take special pride in books they bring to school to share. Make some book bears to help students remember to bring books from home or a library. Use a permanent marker to write a student's name and "Bring a Book" on a strip of poster board. Glue a cute bear-face cutout to the strip. Encourage each child who's given a book bear to have his bear help him find a good book to read. Whenever a book bear shows up with a book, take some time to discuss or read the book.

Foreign Phrases

Your youngsters can take great pride in having learned a foreign language during times that might otherwise have been fairly unproductive. For example, while youngsters are waiting for their turns at the water fountain, they can count softly, "uno, dos, tres, cuatro, cinco, [next person], uno, dos, tres..." In the room they can play Pato, Pato, Ganzo (Duck, Duck, Goose). Children are fascinated by the sounds of a second language and take pride in their progress.

Rexanne Francis—Developmental K, Wayland Union Schools, Wayland, MI

Check It Out!

Michael-Dec 8-<u>Rudolph</u>

~~Kristen-Dec 9-Snowy Day~~

~~Tim-Dec 9-Wake Up Bear~~

Josh-Dec 10-<u>Frederick</u>

Allison-Dec 10-<u>The Night</u>

Check It Out!

This hassle-free system will encourage children to share child-made books and other classroom favorites with their parents. Begin by posting a large piece of chart paper on a wall or countertop. To check a book out, a child prints her name, the date, and the title of her chosen book (in part if necessary) on the chart paper. When the book is returned, the child puts a line through the relevant information on the chart. Once a youngster's name is crossed off the list, she is free to check out another book. What an easy way to promote reading, writing, and the home-school connection. Check it out!

Pat Bollinger
Leopold R-3
Leopold, MO

Read-to-Me Library

If you would like to generate reading enthusiasm, then check this out! Employ a read-to-me library in your classroom. To establish this library system, write the title of each classroom book on an individual index card. Glue a library card pocket to the inside cover of each book; then insert the corresponding index card. Give each student a library card pocket to decorate and label with his name. Mount each personalized pocket on a poster board. Hang the poster on a wall near your classroom library. Have each child choose a book he'd like a family member to read to him. Instruct him to take the card out of the book's pocket and place it in his personalized pocket before taking the book home. Upon returning the book, have each child take the card from his personalized pocket and place it back in the book's pocket. This idea not only teaches youngsters responsibility, but it's also a fun way to involve youngsters' family members.

Jeanne N. Taylor, Cincinnati, OH

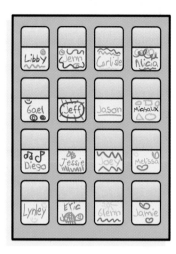

All Join Hands!

Here's an activity that will reinforce listening skills and honor diversity as well as similarities among your students. Begin by seating your children in a circle. Call out a direction such as one of those suggested below. When the specified children stand, ask them to move to the middle of the circle and join hands. Then have them sit down where they are. Repeat this process many times, having children move from group to group. Make your last direction one that will include everyone, such as "Stand if you are a student in [Ms. Wiklendt's] class." Have all the children join hands and form a circle like the one they were in at the beginning of the activity. Guide children to summarize that they are all alike and different in many ways, but they are all part of the same class!

Stand and hold hands if
• you are wearing [sneakers]
• you like [chocolate] ice cream
• you have a [brother]
• you have a [dog]

Jamie Wiklendt, Chattahoochee Elementary, Duluth, GA

Today we went to the music room. We played instruments. Our favorite was the drum.

We read a book about a frog.

"Paws" for the Weekly News

This zoo-themed read-the-room activity is the cat's meow! Choose five children (or groups) to each border a separate sheet of titled chart paper with paw prints. To do this, you might provide sponges and paint, stamps and stamp pads, or colorful markers. As you gather together at the end of each day, invite your class to dictate any newsworthy events from that day. Write their responses on one of the decorated sheets of chart paper. At the end of the week, save the chart paper pages to create meaningful read-the-room activities. First, add a cover page with that week's date; then staple the pages together. Hang each week's pages on a rack so children can practice reading—and read to classroom visitors.

New Twists on Old Sayings

Capture youthful perspectives with refreshing new children's versions of traditional sayings and proverbs. In advance, ask a local framing shop for matting scraps that would normally be discarded. Cut the scraps into squares. Begin by reading, in turn, an incomplete saying or proverb to each child. After pausing a moment for the child to think about her response, have her finish the saying. Noting the child's new ending, type the revised saying on a paper square along with the appropriate byline. Attach the child's saying to a mat square that is a little larger than the paper which bears her saying. Provide glitter, tissue paper, glue, and other miscellaneous supplies; then have each child use the supplies to decorate the exposed mat frame around her saying.

Ann Scalley—Preschool
Wellfleet Preschool
Wellfleet, MA

Got a Minute? Get a Poem

When was the last time you waxed poetic? Keep a few good poem books on hand for this purpose. Select a child to choose the book from which the poem is to be read. Before reading the poem, tell the students its title and author. In no time at all you can convert your youngsters into great lovers of poetry.

Mary Johnson, Grandville Christian School, Grandville, MI

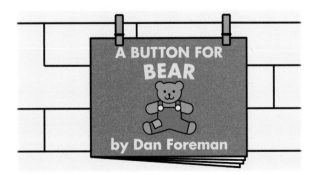

Big Books for Little Hands

Making big books accessible to little hands will be easy with this tip. For each big book you'd like to display, hot-glue two wooden clothespins onto a wall. Then clip the books to the wall. Now all of your big books are easy to view and easy to use!

Esther S. Wert
Children's Place Preschool
Sayre, PA

Jack and Jill went up the hill. What happened to make Jack fall down?

Thinkers

Reserve a portion of your board for a daily creative and critical-thinking activity. Draw or post a humorous character design in the board space reserved for the daily "thinker." Then, in the remaining space, write a thought-provoking question that relates to your weekly theme. During a nursery rhyme unit, for example, you may write something like this: Jack and Jill went up the hill. What happened to make Jack fall down? When you have a little time to spare, ask each youngster to respond to the question. Youngsters will be delighted that all answers are acceptable, and you may be surprised with their divergent thoughts.

Jayne Gammons
Oak Grove Elementary
Durham, NC

Have You Heard This One?

Fill some spare time with children's literature. Encourage children to bring favorite books from home. Then, when time permits, have a child who has a book sit in the teacher's chair and "read" the book to the class. You'll find that sometimes the youngsters' embellished stories are more entertaining than the original ones. Encourage everyone to applaud for a job well done.

Beverly Evans
Pinar Elementary School
Orlando, FL

Mascot's Journal

Imagine the delight of a preschooler who has just learned that the class mascot is going home with him for the evening! When it is a student's turn to take the mascot home, have him place the stuffed animal in a bookbag that has been labeled for this purpose. In the bookbag, include a notebook that contains a note asking parents to help their child make a journal entry, along with a sample entry. Each time the mascot returns to school with a new journal entry, read the entry aloud to the class.

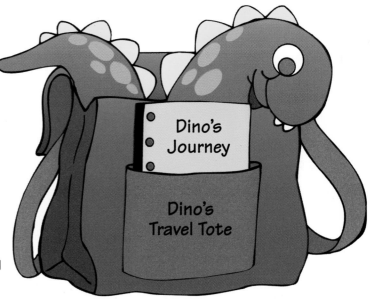

Dino's Journey

Dino's Travel Tote

Find the Pattern

Choose six children who represent a pattern to come to the front of the class. To begin, you may just want to use ABAB patterns. The arrangement could be boy/girl/boy/girl or shirts with buttons/shirts with no buttons/shirts with buttons/shirts with no buttons. The remainder of the class carefully observes the youngsters to determine the pattern. When the pattern is discovered and revealed, choose six more children who represent a different pattern and begin again.

Peg Liebmann, Rockwell School, Fort Atkinson, WI

The Numbers Game

Looking for a math exercise to fill a few minutes? Here's one that little ones will enjoy. Have students stand in a circle. Then have youngsters count off, stopping at a specified number. The child who calls out the specified number sits down. For example, if the specified number is four, youngsters count, "One, two, three, four," and the youngster who said, "four," sits down. The count begins at one again, and play continues in this manner until each youngster is seated.

Bobbie Hallman, Burbank School, Merced, CA

Easy 123s

Wow! This alternative to your traditional number line is really eye-catching! Simply use double-sided tape or Sticky-Tac to attach interlocking foam number squares to your wall. Or hot-glue the squares to the wall if it is a surface from which the glue can later be removed. If you have an incomplete set of numbers, connect the pieces in random order; then attach them to your bathroom walls as a border.

Math

Estimation Chart

Save preparation time with this versatile estimation chart. Leaving the upper one quarter of a poster board sheet blank, print each child's name and draw a space for writing his estimation. (Leave additional room for the names of children who may enroll later.) Laminate the poster board. When you have an estimation assignment for students, write it near the top of the poster using a transparency pen. Write or have each student write his estimate in the space by his name. When youngsters have compared their estimates with the actual figure, the board may be erased for repeated use.

Kendra Olson
Seneca Elementary School
Seneca, IL

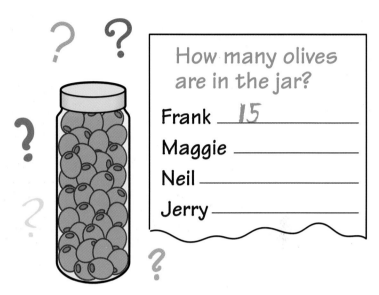

How many olives are in the jar?

Frank _15_
Maggie _____
Neil _____
Jerry _____

How Many?

At a moment's notice you can start this math activity that challenges students' counting skills and increases their awareness of their environment. Ask youngsters "how many" questions. For example, ask, "How many children are wearing red?" Then help youngsters count aloud to verify their responses.

Mary E. Maurer—Preschool
Children's Corner
Caddo, OK

Counter Keepers

Use lids from jumbo crayon boxes to help students keep up with small items. For example, when working with math counters or other small items, have each student manipulate the items in his lid. When using a lid in this manner, each student will not only have his own personal workspace, but the lid will also keep small pieces in place.

Pablo Millares
Van E. Blanton Elementary
Miami, FL

JUMBO CRAYONS

Songbooks

Use this nifty idea to make locating songs, poems, and fingerplays an easy task. Write theme-related songs, poems, and fingerplays on a series of index cards. Laminate the cards. Using a hole puncher, punch two holes at the top of each card; then bind the cards with metal rings to make a book. Provide several blank index cards in each book so you can add to it at a later time. This handy reference will help you find what you need in a hurry.

Jane Walker
Hubbard Elementary
Forsyth, GA

Neon to the Rescue

Use this glowing idea to make locating seasonal songs and fingerplays an easy task. Program neon-colored index cards with your favorite fingerplays, songs, and poems. Use a different color of neon cards for each month or season. For example, use orange cards for October or red cards for February. Keep the cards in an index-file box. This colorful filing system will help you find what you need in a hurry.

Virginia Frehn, Trinity Day Care Preschool, Walnut Bottom, PA

It's in the Bag!

Looking for a fun way to review your favorite classroom songs and fingerplays? If so, this idea is in the bag! In advance, collect your favorite songs and fingerplays. Write a different one on one side of several index cards; then mount a picture cue for each one on the opposite side of the cards. For example, you may write the song "The Wheels on the Bus" on one side of a card and glue a bus cutout to the back of the card. Place all of the index cards in a decorated fabric bag. When you want your little ones to sing or recite fingerplays, have a child pick a card from the bag; then have the class sing or recite what's on the card. Keep adding to your collection throughout the year, and by the end of the year, you'll have a bagful of songs!

Amy Aloi—Head Start
Prince Georges County Head Start
Bladensburg, MD

Berry Basket

Here's an easy way to gather up your youngsters for small-group instruction. Glue a personalized berry cutout onto a clothespin for each child. Clip the clothespins around the edge of a berry basket. As you call out a child's name, put his berry in the basket. Then you can see at a glance who you have yet to see in your small group.

Betty P. Reynolds
Stewartsville Elementary School
Vinton, VA

Cooperative Learning

Teach your older preschoolers this effective way to participate in planned group work. Decide the number of small groups you would like to divide your class into. For each group, prepare a different-shaped group sign. Cut a number of smaller shapes to match the color and shape of each group sign. Then label these smaller shapes with the jobs needed for the group project.

When it is time for group work, place each of the group signs on a different table. Then randomly distribute the smaller shapes labeled with the jobs. Direct each child to use her shape to find the table at which she will be working. Demonstrate how each different job in the project should be done. Then have the groups get busy. Everyone has a job to do!

Suzanne Mayo—Four- and Five-Year-Olds, Pre-K
Our Lady of Peace
Fords, NJ

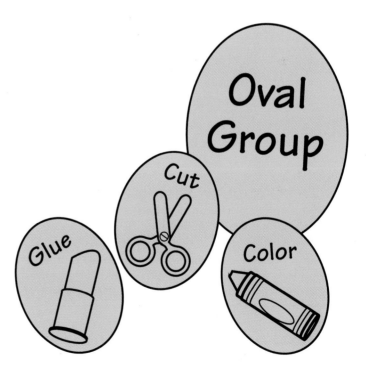

Substitutes

The Packet Option

Realizing that notes from a lesson plan that make perfect sense to one person may mean absolutely nothing to another, give your substitute the packet option. In your lesson plans note that she may complete the lessons according to your plans or she may opt to select from five specially prepared packets of seasonal plans instead. Each packet is based on a theme for the day and includes a daily schedule, important concepts to be covered, and objectives. Some other things to include in each packet are a book with a related activity suggestion, a game such as bingo, and manipulative activities. This system is nice because your substitute can select the option she likes best, because you'll be covered for up to five school days, and because the packets can be easily refilled to be used again during the next school year.

Ann Rowe
Western Hills Elementary
Omaha, NE

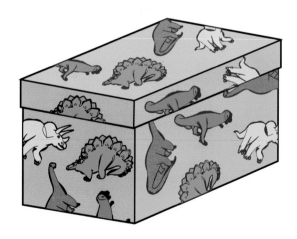

Sticker Treats

Help your substitute teacher get off on a positive start with your youngsters. Supply her with stickers and encourage her to award them to youngsters for positive behaviors. Immediately she'll begin looking for the things that they are doing right.

Jill DeMarchi
Carnelian School
Alta Loma, CA

Dinosaur Theme Box

Your youngsters will know they're in for a "dino-mite" day when your substitute teacher hauls out the dinosaur box! Cover a lidded box with dinosaur gift wrap or self-adhesive covering. Fill the box with several days' worth of dinosaur ideas and the materials and resources for carrying them out. Also include the classroom schedules and other information your substitute will need. Your youngsters will appreciate the change of pace and the fun-filled topic. And your substitute will appreciate not having to scramble around looking for supplies.

Ann Marie Lake
Woodland Academy
Ware, MA

Multiple Classes

If you teach more than one group of children, a substitute's job can be particularly challenging. Simplify her task by assigning each group a sticker symbol (star, sun, or moon, for example). Use these stickers to label each group's cubbies, storage shelves, and supplies. Label a folder with the symbol for each group. To the inside front cover of each, attach a schedule and class list. Also include the appropriate quantity of any paper supplies and notes to parents that each group will need. After identifying the materials for each group in this manner, a substitute's job will seem much less confusing.

Joyce Eggebeen
Oostburg, WI

Now Hear This!

Need to leave plans for a substitute teacher on really short notice? Try this clever little shortcut. Record your instructions on an audiocassette rather than taking the time to write everything down. Also record a message for your youngsters so that they'll know why you're away and when you'll be back. Rewind the tape and place a tape player with the cued tape on your desktop along with a note that says, "Now hear this!" You may be surprised to find that you can relay all the information necessary in a fraction of the time it would have taken to write it.

Sandra Whalen
Odom Elementary
Austin, TX

Substitutes

More Than Just a Pretty Package

Although you can package these supplies for lots of eye appeal, your substitute teacher may find the package to be among the most practical of all surprises. Select four favorite children's books. With each book, package a related whole-language activity suggestion (with the necessary supplies) and a related art suggestion (with the necessary supplies). Also include in the box a puppet, stickers, activity sheets, a bingo game, copies of fingerplays and rhymes, and a tape of favorite children's songs. With all these fun things to choose from, it's possible your youngsters won't even know you're gone.

Jane Coldiron
Centerville Elementary
Suwanee, GA

Lesson Plan Lifesaver

At 6:00 A.M., this technique is truly a lifesaver. Write your classroom schedule and procedures, leaving spaces to insert daily lesson plans. Then laminate the schedule and keep it at home. When a substitute is needed on short notice, use an overhead projector pen to quickly jot down substitute-friendly lesson plans in the blank spaces of the laminated schedule. Once this schedule has served its purpose, wipe off the programming and take it home to be used again—heaven forbid.

Sandra Sizemore, College Park Elementary School, Virginia Beach, VA

Have a question? Call one of these helpful volunteers!

Jenn Teester   555-1524
Liz Hayworth   555-3657
Carlisle Brown   555-8876

Voluntary Assistants

If you have adult classroom volunteers who can be helpful to a substitute teacher, give her their names and phone numbers. Or arrange for one of them to be on stand-by in case your substitute should need an extra hand. Having someone around who knows how your classroom usually operates can be a tremendous help to someone who has just stepped into your classroom for the first time.

Linda Schwitzke—Preschool, Head Start
Longview, WA

Pack It in a Box

Employ this personal management technique, and you'll never have to fret about an unexpected absence. As a habit, plan activities at least one week in advance. Reproduce any papers you'll be using and make up samples of projects in advance. Then file the papers and the samples in a desktop box of six file folders. Label each of five of the folders with a different day of the week. Label the sixth folder "weekly work." In this folder store your weekly lesson plans, seating chart, and teacher's copies of daily assignments. In each of the five daily folders, include lists of materials needed for activities and the locations of the supplies.

Heidi Weber—Preschool
Hyde Park Playschool
Cincinnati, OH

Songs for the Substitute

Round up the words to your students' favorite songs, so your substitute teacher can lead youngsters in songs during transition times or conduct a sing-along. Write or photocopy favorite fingerplays and holiday songs onto index cards. Punch a hole in the upper left corner of each card. Separate the songs by month if desired; then bind each month's cards on a metal ring. Display these rings in a prominent location. Whether it's you or your substitute who's reaching for the ring, it'll be great to have this convenient resource at your fingertips.

Linda Parr—Pre/K, Lakeland Elementary, Coldwater, MI

A Moving Picture Is Worth a Million Words

If there is such a thing as a "normal day," and if you can capture it on videotape, you'll never have to worry about an uninformed substitute again. Narrate a videotape in which you record your class involved in typical classroom routines. Include a segment that shows a substitute teacher where to look for the supplies and information she will need during the day. And, if desired, have each youngster introduce himself on tape. After viewing and editing the tape, place it and lesson plans where they can be located quickly whenever a substitute is required. After taking just a few minutes to view the tape (with your youngsters if necessary), your substitute can see for herself how to proceed. If a picture is worth a thousand words, a moving picture is worth a million words.

Carrie Herder, Blessed Sacrament School, Milwaukee, WI

Substitutes

Mr. Who

With Mr. Who by her side, your substitute teacher can begin immediately to call on children by name. Attach an owl cutout to a small container. Label the owl "Mr. Who," and then cover the container with clear Con-Tact covering. Inside the container, place cards each of which bears a different youngster's name. When your substitute wants participation, all she needs to do is reach inside the container, take out a card, and call the child whose name is on it. By using all the cards before replacing any, she can be sure to include every child. Mr. Who may be so popular that you'll want to use him yourself.

Brenda Purvis
Asheville Christian Academy
Asheville, NC

Substitute Teacher Booklet

If you're one of those people who prefers to be prepared at every moment, then you may be most comfortable with a booklet. Pull together all the information a substitute teacher could need. Include lunch count and attendance procedures, meal and snack routines, emergency plans, resource class information, schedules, and dismissal procedures. Ask your school secretary to file one copy of this booklet in the office and store the other one in your top desk drawer. Now you're ready!

Kay Tidwell
Savoy Independent School District
Savoy, TX

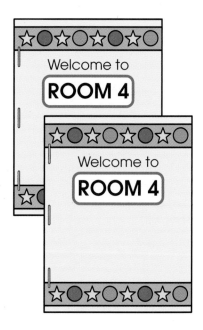

Welcome to
ROOM 4

Welcome to
ROOM 4

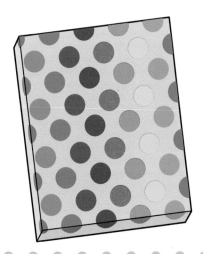

Surprise, Surprise, Surprise!

If you're planning your absence, plan to surprise and delight your youngsters with an end-of-the-day treat. Wrap up a new book, a tasty treat, or a new game for the occasion. Direct your substitute teacher to produce it near the end of the day. For those little ones who are missing their teacher, this is a great way to brighten the day.

Joan Adams
Creative Learning Center
Montgomery, AL

Arts and Crafts

Contents

Displaying

An Art Collection

Use this method for saving student artwork throughout the year, and you'll be ready at a moment's notice for an end-of-the-year art show. Each time you do art projects in the classroom, save two students' work. Indicate on a class checklist which students have had artwork chosen. Continue in this manner until you have at least two pieces of artwork from each child. You won't be rushing to collect artwork at the end of the year, and you'll have a good representation of the year's projects. On with the show!

Deborah Pruett—Preschool
St. Mary of the Woods College, Woods Preschool
St. Mary of the Woods, IN

Easy Art Easel and Art Display

Got a clip? Use this tip! Use large plastic spring clips (such as those used to clip potato chip bags closed) to create instant easels and displays. Just nail each clip within student reach into a wooden surface, such as a thin piece of plywood, a wall, or the side of a wooden cabinet or shelf. Invite a student to slip a piece of art paper into the clip for an instant easel or hang his work from a clip for display.

Gayle J. Vergara—Preschool
Willowbend Preschool
Murrieta, CA

Displaying

Why Would They Do That?

Often, teachers display samples of students' artwork. But sometimes it's difficult for a parent to look at an art project and know the education-related aspects of completing the project. So when you display crafts or artwork, also display an information sheet that tells parents some of the learning experiences students may have had while completing this artwork and that lists other experiences tied in with this activity.

Kay Thomas—Preschool, Bradley United Methodist Preschool, Greenfield, IN

Craft: Jointed Teddy Bear

Skills: cutting, tying, red, brown

Related activity: making small teddy bear puppets

Story: Teddy Bears' Picnic by Jimmy Kennedy

Snack: Picnic with snack lunch and pink lemonade

Hanging Art

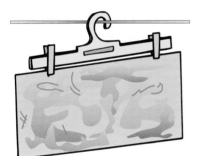

Need a helpful hint for moving students' wet paintings from one place to another? If so, then try this neat idea. Clip a sheet of art paper to each of several clip-style hangers. Place the hangers in your painting center on a tension rod or clothes-drying rack. Encourage each youngster who visits the center to place the hook of a hanger over the top of the paint easel. After he paints on the paper, have him hang the picture up to dry. Using this technique is a great way to display artwork while keeping little fingers clean.

Michelle Miget—Four-Year-Olds
Humboldt Elementary Preschool, St. Joseph, MO

Learned in Kindergarten

This end-of-the-year display is a great review of the artwork your students have done during the year. Throughout the year, ask for a different student to donate his finished artwork for display each time a project is finished. Or, if you return a lot of projects to them at the end of the year, have students volunteer selected pieces from their collections. On a bulletin board, display the sampling of projects around a copy of Robert Fulghum's poem "All I Really Need to Know I Learned in Kindergarten." Youngsters will enjoy the display because it naturally encourages them to reminisce about the topics they've covered during the year. Preschoolers who come to school to register for the following year will be delighted at this evidence of all the learning fun that awaits them.

Sheryl Nash
Liverpool Elementary School
Liverpool, NY

All I Really Need to Know I Learned in Kindergarten

All I really need to know I learned in kindergarten.

Displaying

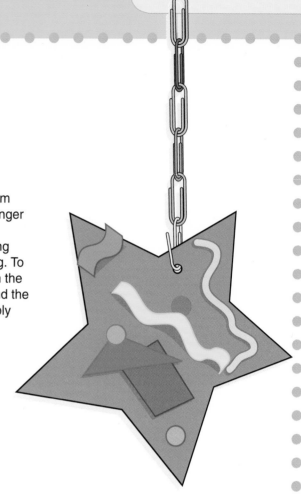

Clip Hangers

Are you on the edge of your seat looking for more classroom display space? Link up with this clip hanging idea! Make a hanger for each child by linking a series of large colored paper clips together. Slide one end of each hanger under a different ceiling tile or hang it from a self-adhesive hook attached to the ceiling. To display a child's work, simply slide it into the last paper clip on the hanger. For heavier work, punch a hole in the project and bend the last paper clip so that it will hook through that hole. Then simply hang around!

Dayle Timmons
Alimacani Elementary School
Jacksonville, FL

Helping Hands

Do you ever feel like you need extra hands to help you display students' work? If so, this idea will come in handy. Laminate a class supply of construction paper hand shapes. Personalize a hand shape for each child in your class; then hot-glue a clothespin to the back of each one. Attach each hand to a wall in your classroom by hot-gluing the clothespin to the wall at a child's eye level. (Hot glue may damage wallboard.) When a child has a project to display, have him press on his hand shape to open the clothespin, then insert his work. Look what little hands can do!

Tina Mrozek—Three-Year-Olds
Childrens World Learning Center
Westmont, IL

Adam

Art Clips

Use clothesline and clothes-pins to eliminate the need for labeling students' artwork. Write each student's name on an individual clothespin and store the clothespins in a basket. Suspend a clothesline at your youngsters' eye level. As each child finishes a project, have him locate his clothespin and clip his artwork to the clothesline. Artwork is quickly labeled and students improve their name recognition skills with ease.

Mary Jo Morrissey—PreK
Preschool Playhouse—YMCA
Little Falls, NY

Can You Label This?

Do your students have difficulty labeling odd-textured, 3-D art projects? Here's a quick solution to that problem. In advance, prepare several self-sticking name labels for each child in your class. Then, when that unusual project needs a label, just peel and stick! This helps identify each child's work without having to wait for an adult to do the writing.

Robin Gorman, Potterville Elementary, Potterville, MI

Project Tablecloth

Some art projects can be difficult to label with a child's name—such as painted rocks or other objects. If you are planning such a project, prevent mix-ups with this idea. Purchase an inexpensive plastic, flannel-backed tablecloth. Use a permanent marker to divide the tablecloth into sections; then write a different child's name in each section. Place each child's project in his section on the tablecloth until it is time to take it home or until you can easily write his name on the project. Now your little artists are sure to take home their own masterpieces!

Barbara Flynn—PreK, St. Raphael School, Bridgeport, CT

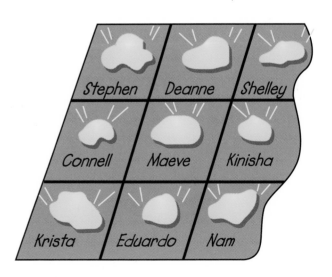

Wonderful Windows

Not enough space for easels in your classroom? Then make use of classroom windows that are at children's level. Simply tape art paper to the window, set the paint on the window's ledge, and let the painting begin! Students will love the view, and you'll love cleaning up with just a wipe of a wet washcloth. Painting without easels is easy!

Amanda Brown and Diane McKinney—Two- and
  Three-Year-Olds
A Child's View
Newton, NC

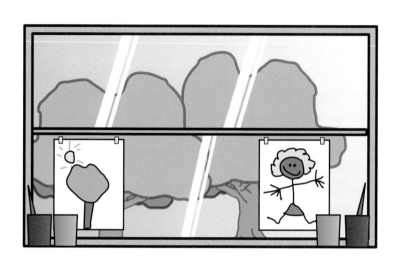

Paint-Pot Liners

Does the cleaning of paint pots have you pooped? If so, use this timesaving alternative. Insert one plastic sandwich bag into each paint pot. Fold the plastic over the rim of the pot and secure it with either the inner lid or a rubber band. Fill the pot with paint. When the paint pot is empty, just pull out the plastic bag and replace it with another one. Refill and paint!

Karen Bryant and Robin Walker—PreK
Miller Elementary
Warner Robins, GA

Paint Storage Solution

Storing paint at your easel couldn't be easier when you have baby bottles do the dirty work. Simply collect a five-ounce plastic baby bottle (with a cap) for each color of paint. Fill each bottle half full, tighten the cap, and place the bottles in your easel trays. When it's time to paint, remove the plastic caps and insert a paintbrush into each bottle. At cleanup time, replace the caps and wash the brushes. When the bottles need cleaning, just put them in the dishwasher. No mess, no fuss!

Angie Eberspacher—Preschool
Beaver Crossing, NE

Reusable Tubs

Use individual-serving applesauce tubs to distribute individual portions of paint or short crayon stubs. The tubs last well and are just the right size for little fingers.

Jill Beattie, Wilson College Child Care, Chambersburg, PA

Half-Pints of Paint

If your classroom sink is constantly filled with paint cups that need washing, then this tip is for you! Open the top of an empty half-pint milk carton; then fill the carton with paint. Keep the paint fresh for weeks by using a clothespin to close the carton when not in use. When the carton is empty, simply toss it in the trash can. You'll never wash paint cups again!

Carole Tobisch, Denmark Early Childhood Center
Denmark, WI

Colorful Paintbrushes

Get a handle on messy paint centers with this colorful suggestion. Use enamel paint to paint the handles of brushes and the paint cups in matching colors. Fill each cup with its corresponding color of paint. As students paint their masterpieces, they'll be able to replace the brushes in the correct cups by matching the colors.

Vickie Zalk—Three-Year-Olds
Hope Creative Preschool
Winter Haven, FL

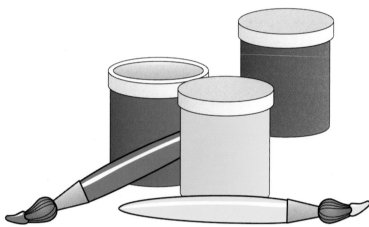

Disappearing Clutter

You will see all that unwanted can clutter disappear when you use this attractive idea for storing powdered tempera paint. Simply pour each color of paint into a different transparent plastic freezer container. Be sure the lids are sealed properly; then stack them in nice, neat rows. Now you see it; now you don't!

Teri Walker, Moline Elementary, Moline, KS

Recycled Paint Cups

Don't throw away those wonderfully sturdy, plastic frosting containers! They make great paint cups for your easel. To make one, use a craft knife to cut a paintbrush hole in the lid of the container. Then pour paint into the container, snap on the lid, insert the brush, and it's ready for action!

Teresa Edison—Four- and Five-Year-Olds
Luther Hospital Child Care Center
Eau Claire, WI

Handy Holders

Make painting easier for little ones by using an individual serving–size applesauce container to hold each block of compressed tempera paint. You'll find that youngsters manipulate a container better than a whole tray, and you can determine how many colors are available for any given project. How do you get a supply of these handy holders? Have applesauce for a snack one day. Little ones will enjoy eating the contents to empty the containers for you!

Cindy S. Berry—Two-Year-Olds
Christian Kindergarten and Nursery School
Little Rock, AR

Slip-Slidin' Away

Help prevent accidental spills from paint containers that easily slide on slippery surfaces. Obtain a roll of Rubbermaid Grip Liner. Cut the pebbly, rubber cupboard liner to match the shapes of the bottoms of your paint containers; then adhere the liner to the containers. Or cut the liner into sections that can be adhered to a tabletop. Then set each container onto the section of liner. What a great way to keep everything in its place!

Mary Jenks—Preschool Special Education–Hearing Impaired
Briarlake Elementary
Decatur, GA

Easel Options

Need more easel space in your classroom? Try this easy easel option. Begin by attaching Con-Tact covering to a low bulletin board or wall. For each art space that you'd like to have, hot-glue two spring-type clothespins to the background as shown. Provide art supplies in shoeboxes or plastic window boxes on the floor. Also keep a supply of art paper nearby. To work in this area, a child simply hangs a sheet of art paper from two clothespins, and the scene is set for creativity.

Patricia Parahus—PreK
Our Redeemer School
Levittown, NY

Management

Yarn Dispenser

Keep the yarn at your art center tangle free with this idea. Place a ball of yarn in a plastic berry basket and then thread one end of the yarn through a hole in the basket. Next, place a pair of child-safe scissors in the basket with the yarn. To use the dispenser, pull the desired amount of yarn through the hole. Then use the scissors to cut the yarn so that a short length still remains threaded through the hole. The ball of yarn stays in place and stays neatly rolled!

Suzanne Maki—PreK, Fuller Head Start, Gloucester, MA

Grinning About Glitter

Glitter is great to use on art projects, but can be grisly at cleanup time. To get a grip on glitter, use pie pans. When a child wishes to use glitter on a craft project, have him place his project in a pie pan. As he shakes glitter onto his project, the excess glitter will fall into the pan. At the end of the art activity, pour the glitter in the pan back into the bottle. With this tip, glitter will make you grin again!

Carole Watkins—PreK
Holy Family Child Care Center
Crown Point, IN

Glitter Gel

Glitter projects sure look great, but they leave such a mess! Use this idea to help eliminate the glitter litter in your classroom. Mix one cup of glitter with one-third cup of inexpensive hair gel. Then use a paintbrush to brush a thin layer of the mixture onto an art project. The gel will dry clear, and the glitter will adhere to the project.

Vicki Ingram—PreK, Ventura Missionary Preschool
Ventura, CA

Glitter Containers

Put a little sparkle into your art projects with this helpful hint. Use empty spice containers to hold glitter. Youngsters can sprinkle the amount of glitter needed for art projects, and the containers are just the right size for little hands.

Kelly Beach, Kelly's Kids, Leesburg, FL

Storage Buckets

Organize your craft supplies and end closet clutter with this neat idea. Collect a supply of plastic, gallon-size ice-cream buckets. Label each bucket to identify its contents. Store items such as fabric scraps, cotton balls, craft sticks, pipe cleaners, and construction paper scraps in these nifty containers.

Chris Garchow—PreK, St. Paul's Lutheran School Janesville, WI

Mr. Glue, Ms. Scissors, and The Happy Crayons

Introduce your youngsters to these characters and they're sure to remember how to use glue, scissors, and crayons appropriately. To prepare, glue wiggle eyes on a bottle of glue, a pair of scissors, and several crayons. Introduce each character or group of characters individually; then use the characters again whenever a reminder is needed. Here are some things the characters might say to help your children use these art materials.

Teena Perry—Preschool, Rainbow Bears Preschool, Oklahoma City, OK

Mr. Glue:
This is my hat (point to orange cap), my head (point to rim of bottle), and my tummy (point to the body of the bottle). To open me, twist my hat this way (demonstrate). I like it when people squeeze my tummy so softly that you can hear and feel me breathe (squeeze the bottle next to each child so he can hear and feel the air going in and out of the bottle). If you squeeze me gently, I will put small drops of glue on your project (demonstrate). Please do not squeeze my tummy too hard. When you are finished, twist my hat back on this way (demonstrate).

The Happy Crayons: The paper wrapped around us keeps us strong. Please do not pull off our papers! Please be careful not to squeeze us too hard or rub us on paper too hard because we might break. Ouch! When you are finished with us, please put us back in our happy home (put crayons back in box or basket) so we do not get lonely or roll away and get lost.

Ms. Scissors:
This is my head (point to handle) and this is my mouth (open and close blades). When you carry me, hold my mouth closed so that my teeth don't hurt anyone (demonstrate). If you want to use me, put your thumb in the top of my head and three of your fingers in the bottom of my head (demonstrate). When you are using me to cut, open my mouth wide like this so that I take big bites or open my mouth just a little bit like this so that I take small bites (demonstrate).

Management

In the Bag

Here's an arts-and-crafts management tip to help you spend less time handing out art materials and more time assisting young artists with their work. In advance, prepare a resealable plastic bag for each student. In the bag, include the materials needed to complete one project. Simply give a bag to each child when it is time for art; then collect the empty bags and use them again another day.

Sally Bankson—PreK
Heritage Christian School
Bothell, WA

Craft Caddy

Looking for a sturdy carryall for scissors, paintbrushes, markers, and the like? Try a silverware caddy from a dishwasher! The compartments will help organize tools and craft items, and little ones love to carry the caddy by the handle. If it gets dirty, just pop it in the dishwasher!

Nancy Goldberg—Three-Year-Olds
B'nai Israel Schilit Nursery School
Rockville, MD

Paper Scrap Pails

Here's a neat tip for collecting paper scraps. Place one plastic sand pail on each table. Throughout the day, have youngsters discard paper scraps in the pail. At the end of each day, designate one child from each table to empty the pail into your scrap-paper box. Then you'll have a supply of paper scraps whenever you need them.

Mildred W. Hill
Eastside Elementary
Coweta County, GA

Crayon Container

Keep those crayons in the right hands by storing crayons in small Crystal Light drink containers (0.99 oz.). To make individual containers, cut each can to the height of the crayons. Write the child's name in marker on a piece of masking tape and place it on the side of the can. This crayon organizational method allows the children to practice recognizing their names and to be responsible for their own crayons.

Renee Culver—PreK
Ginger Bread House Day Care
Peoria Heights, IL

Glamorous Glue

Use nail-polish bottles instead of glue bottles to give little ones more success with gluing activities. Clean empty nail-polish bottles and brushes with nail-polish remover, rinse them in water, and let them dry. Then fill the bottles with glue. Fine-motor skills are exercised as a child uses the nail brush to apply glue to his projects. Rub cooking oil on the brushes periodically to keep them soft. A glamour tip from the pros—less is more!

Kitty Moufarrege—Three-Year-Olds
Foothill Progressive Montessori Preschool
La Canada, CA

Sticky Solution!

It's true! You really can keep freshly glued or painted projects from sticking together when you try this simple tip! Just stock your art center with several pieces of waxed paper. Each time a child completes a project that needs to dry, have her layer it between two pieces of waxed paper. Once the project is dry, simply remove the waxed paper. No mess. No fuss. Just smooth-looking art!

Lynn Coleman—Preschool
Tumbling Tykes Preschool
Endwell, NY

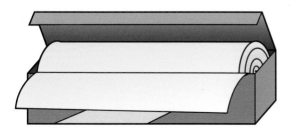

Management

Glue Stamp Pad

Need a neat way for little ones to apply glue? If so, then try this nifty idea. Place a soft kitchen sponge in a plastic container; then pour glue onto the sponge. After the glue soaks into the sponge, have a youngster press the item that needs glue onto the sponge. Place a lid on the container when it's not in use and it will be ready again for next time.

Pattie Sigmon—Four- and Five-Year-Olds
Triplett Child Development
Mooresville, NC

Glue-Be-Gone

Here's a way to keep glue-bottle caps from sticking to the bottle. After twisting the cap to open the bottle for the first time, use a cotton swab to apply a small amount of petroleum jelly to the bottom of the dispenser shaft under the cap. The glue cap will easily twist to open and close the bottle!

Carleen Coderre—Preschool
Bright Beginnings Child Care Center, Three Rivers, MA

No-Spill Glue

Do you have "no-spill" paint cups in your room? In addition to filling them with paint, fill some of them with glue. It's easy to squirt glue in the holes in the rims and the snap-on lids keep the glue from drying out. Best of all, children can use paintbrushes to apply glue to their projects so that there's less mess! Storage is easy, too. Just stack 'em up!

Ellyn Soypher—Preschool
Chizuk Amuno Preschool
Baltimore, MD

No More Paste Problems

Put an end to messy paste jars. Plastic 35mm film canisters make great individual paste containers. The lids snap on tight to keep the paste from drying out, and they're just the right size for little fingers. These canisters are easy to store and make for an easy cleanup.

Debbie Buckley
Broadmoor Elementary School
Lafayette, LA

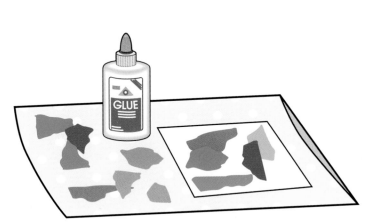

A Cleaning Dream

If gluing activities leave you with sticky tables, try this unique solution. Use old pillowcases as children's work mats. When finished with the activity, simply shake off excess art materials and toss the pillowcases in the wash. Cleanup is a dream!

Lori Kracoff—Preschool
The Curious George Cottage Learning Center
Waterville Valley, NH

Handy Hang-Ups

Put an end to paint-smock clutter and assist your little ones in being successful "hanger-uppers" with this catchy idea. Affix the hook side of a long strip of Velcro to a wall near your easel area. Attach the loop side of a piece of Velcro to the collar of each painting smock. To hang up her smock, a child presses the Velcro on the collar to the Velcro strip on the wall. She'll feel independent, and you'll be rewarded with a neat and tidy art area!

Patricia Carpentier
Cedar Grove, WI

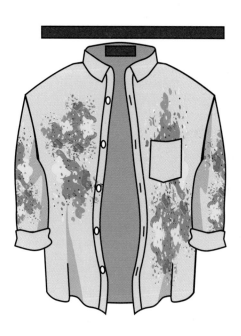

Management

Easy Paint Cleanup
Paint cleanup is a breeze when you "leave it 'til tomorrow." Spoon small amounts of paint onto plastic lids for children's use. Afterward, lay the lids in an out-of-the-way place to dry. The following morning, just tap the lids on the inside edge of a wastebasket and the leftover paint pops right out!

Marlene Kimmell
Graysville Elementary School
Graysville, IN

Armed With Socks!
Here's a great way to keep children's shirtsleeves dry and clean while they're playing at the water table, washing their hands at the sink, or painting at easels. Cut the elastic bands from the tops of old tube socks. Slip one band onto each of a child's arms so that the bands hold up loose sleeves and act as a protective layer between the water or paint and the child's shirt. Sock bands are quick, easy, and in plentiful supply—so sock it to 'em!

Pat Johnson—Three-Year-Olds
Church of the Redeemer Preschool
Columbus, OH

Tabletop Drop Cloths

Protect tabletops from messy paint drips and splatters with this quick solution. Before your youngsters paint, cover each of your tabletops with an old vinyl tablecloth. To clean up, just fold and store the tablecloths. Each time you use a tablecloth, it will collect more colorful paint splotches as it minimizes messes.

Deanna Whitford
Holt Elementary
Kearney, MO

Tickets, Please!

Use this idea to promote your children's responsibility in keeping the classroom clean and orderly. After a creative art session, ask each child to pick up a piece of paper from the floor. Explain that each piece is a ticket, and that each child will need a ticket in order to join the group's next activity. When scraps are at their worst, request two or more tickets. Tidy up in no time!

Jennifer Barton, Elizabeth Green School, Newington, CT

Clean as a Whistle

Here's a tip that will help finger-paint wash away cleanly and easily. Rub a small amount of petroleum jelly on little hands prior to painting.

Vail McCole—PreK, Tiger's Treehouse
Grand Junction, CO

Management

Smock Frock

Cut back on paint smock expenses with this thrifty idea. To make one, cut out a rectangle from an old vinyl shower curtain or tablecloth. (Adjust the size according to your children's needs.) Then, in the middle of the piece, cut a hole large enough for a child to slip his head through. Keep these smock frocks in your art area where they can easily (and independently!) be slipped on and off.

Peggy L. Emde—Preschool
Kids Under Construction, Inc.
Stillwater, OK

Easy Paint Cleanup

Paint cleanup will be a breeze when using this terrific tip. Cut sheets of bulletin board paper identical in size to your painting easels. Laminate the sheets of paper; then mount one sheet of laminated paper on the front of each easel. Clip art paper to the easels for youngsters to use for painting. After painting, remove the art paper and use a damp cloth to wipe off any excess paint from the laminated paper. What an easy cleanup!

Pam Williams, James E. Bacon Elementary
Jesup, GA

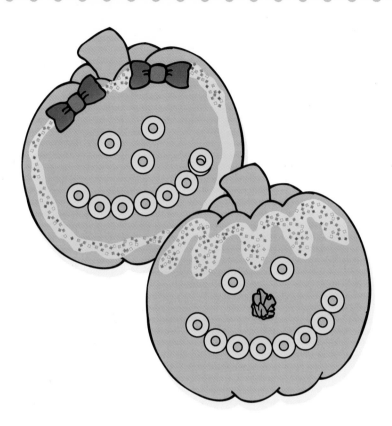

"Deck-orate" the Halls!

When your students partner with their parents, your halls will be decked to the nines—all year round! Near the end of each month, duplicate a class supply of a seasonal shape or an enlarged copy of clip art for each child. Send the shapes/designs home along with a note asking parents to help their children decorate them as desired. They can use Cheerios cereal, ribbon, glitter glue, tissue paper—anything goes! When youngsters return their projects, display these festive, family-made projects along a hallway. Each time parents visit, they'll know they helped make your hall shine throughout every season.

Judy Clifford, Central Elementary
Point Pleasant, WV

A "Sun-sational" Class

This cheerful puzzle display is perfect for reinforcing class spirit and teamwork! Begin by cutting a very large circle from yellow bulletin board paper. With a black marker, draw a smaller circle in the center and write "Our 'Sun-sational' Class" inside it. On the outer circle, draw a sun ray for each child. (Be sure to vary the outer lines of each ray so that each piece will fit in only one place.) Cut apart the rays and give one to each child. Invite each child to decorate his ray with a variety of art supplies. When all the rays are decorated and dry, display them on the floor with the sun center. Encourage small groups of children to take turns working on this giant floor puzzle. When each group has had an opportunity to assemble the puzzle, post it on your classroom door.

Barbara Spilman Lawson, Waynesboro, VA

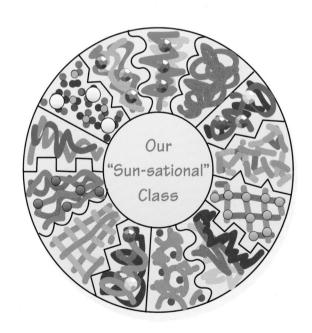

Our "Sun-sational" Class

Projects

Beautiful Bathroom

If your classroom bathroom is nothing to brag about, consider drafting the assistance of parent volunteers to turn it into a dream bath. After obtaining the necessary permission, ask parents to plan a scene for the bathroom walls; then work together to paint the room and add embellishments. Holographic or glow-in-the-dark cutouts, such as stars, may be used to give the bath a truly unique aura. Soon your little ones will be looking forward to the adventure of going to the bathroom.

Sonia M. Sims—PreK/Even Start
Parent & Child Co-op, Engelwood Elementary School
Orlando, FL

Family Pennants

Three cheers for our families! Give each child a pennant-shaped piece of construction paper to decorate at home. Along with the pennant, send a note asking the child's parents to help convert the pennant into a work of art that represents their family. In the note, suggest that the pennant might be decorated with things such as family photos or the handprints of family members. Prominently display each of the pennants when it is returned to school. Soon lots of little ones will be crowded around. There's my family's pennant!

Beth Lemke, Heights Head Start, Coon Rapids, MN

Contents

Good Behavior

A Smooth Ride for Mrs. Ryan's Class

1. Keep your hands and feet to yourself.

2. Follow directions.

3. Be kind.

4. Ask for help when you need it.

A Smooth Ride

As you begin your first few days together as a class, facilitate a discussion encouraging children to think of ways that would enable everyone in the class to work and play well together. As a group, decide what you would like your class rules to be. Emphasize that when everyone follows the rules, things in your classroom are likely to be much more fun for everyone—a smooth ride! Write the rules on a sheet of chart paper. Then enlarge and duplicate the car pattern on page 71. Write a title on the car such as the one shown; then cut it out. Attach the car cutout to the top of your list of rules and post the chart in a prominent place in your classroom.

A Whale of a Big Deal

Before leaving school prior to a planned absence, draw a giant whale on your bulletin board with colorful chalk. Print "We're having a whale of a day!" on the whale. Leave the substitute teacher a note asking her to commend youngsters for their helpfulness, courteousness, and good behavior. When a youngster is complimented, ask her to have him sign his name on or near the whale so that you can hear all about it when you return.

Diane Warrick
Evergreen Elementary School
Midlothian, VA

We're having a whale of a day!

Eric
Mia
Darrell
Jason
Sarah

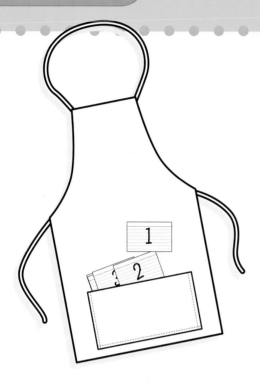

Take a Number, Please

Here's a management technique that promotes patience and teaches numeration at the same time. To help children wait their turns for your individual attention, label as many as five index cards each with a different numeral from one to five. Put the cards in order; then store them in a place that is easy for youngsters to access, such as the front pocket of your apron. When a child needs help, ask him to take a number! Who's next?

Karen Sheheane—Preschool
Killearn United Methodist Preschool
Tallahasee, FL

Shh...

Try this unique idea if you need a quiet room. Very softly say, "If you hear me, wiggle your toes." Then whisper, "If you hear me, touch your nose." Continue with similar directions until everyone is participating. Shh...you won't hear a sound.

Niki Huff—PreK, Stilwell United Methodist Preschool, Belton, MO

Red Light/Green Light Necklace

Do your little ones interrupt when you're working with other children? If so, don a red light/green light necklace. To make a necklace, cut one red and one green construction paper rectangle that are identical in size. Glue the rectangles back-to-back; then laminate them. Punch a hole near one end of the rectangle. Insert yarn through the hole and tie the yarn to make a necklace. Explain to students that the green side represents a green light. When it shows, they can approach you for help. The red side represents a red light. When it shows, students must wait until later to ask for help. Use this easy management system as a helpful reminder for your little ones.

Michele Garza
Whitney Elementary
Whitney, TX

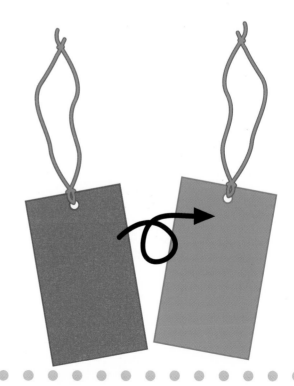

Good Behavior

A Bubble Gum Bonus

Inspire youngsters with this motivational bubble gum display. For each child, cut a bubble gum machine shape from construction paper. Label each cutout with a child's name. Laminate the cutouts if desired. Then post them on a classroom wall. When you spy a child exhibiting good behavior or achieving a goal, reward him with a round sticker to attach to his bubble gum machine. When his machine is full, have him take it home to show his family.

Roxann Reed—Preschool
Tri-City Christian School
Lee's Summit, MO

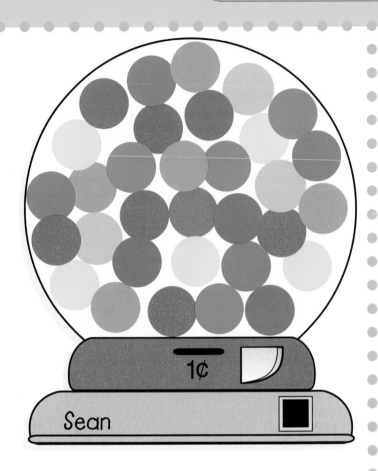

Magic Words

Ordinary words can work magic! At the beginning of the year, select a pair of words (such as *chocolate* and *vanilla* or *peanut butter* and *jelly*) and inform youngsters that these words will be the magic words. When you (or another adult) say the first magic word, youngsters turn to face you and then freeze and listen to your directions. When you're finished giving directions, say the second word. This word signals youngsters to resume working. Each time the class responds appropriately to the magic words, drop a token into a jar. When the jar is full, reward youngsters with a special treat. It's magic!

Pamela Green
Fishburn Park Elementary
Roanoke, VA

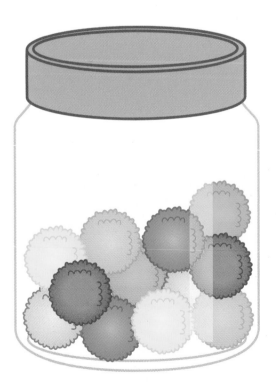

Dual-Purpose Nametags

Use this suggestion and you'll be helping your substitute with name recognition and encouraging good behavior. Make a nametag for each youngster. Punch a hole at the top of each nametag and insert a safety pin. Place these nametags where your substitute will find them. Leave her a note asking her to place one of the stickers you've provided on the back of the tag of each youngster who was helpful and cooperative. When you return, you can take a quick look at the backs of the nametags and commend the youngsters who had a great day in your absence.

Estella Trigo
West Elementary
Levelland, TX

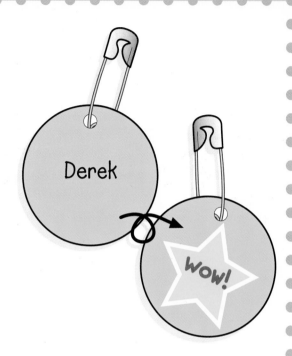

Tickets Up

Here's a positive way to help monitor your classroom noise level. When you say, "Tickets up," have each youngster put his index finger on his closed mouth without talking. This method gives little hands and little lips an active role in being quiet and they'll be proud of their accomplishment. Ah, the silence!

Rita East, Kiddie Kampus Kindergarten, Barling, AR

The Magic Door

Keep hallway chatter down to a minimum with this magical idea. Tell your students to pretend that the doorway from your classroom to the hall is magic and when you step through it, you lose your voice. Model this behavior by moving your lips but not speaking. You'll be amazed just how quiet the hallways are once your youngsters are under the spell of the magical doorway.

Marci Reimer-Haber
Ross Elementary School
Nashville, TN

Good Behavior

An "Egg-cellent" Motivator

Try this "egg-ceptional" idea to promote good behavior. Cut out a quantity of different-colored construction paper eggs. Throughout the day, when a student exhibits positive behavior, give him an egg and ask him to write his name on it. At the end of the day, each student with an egg can redeem it for a chocolate one.

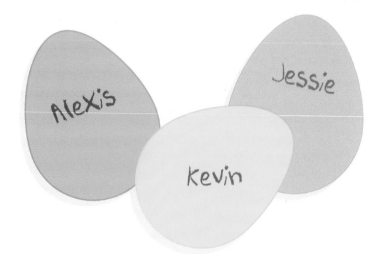

Silent Fingerplays

Waiting in a hallway with a group of preschoolers can be a real challenge, especially if it's necessary to keep the noise level down. The next time this situation arises, silently mouth the words to a fingerplay or song and make the corresponding movements. Soon each of your youngsters will silently join in. Congratulate yourselves on a job well done by clapping with two fingers on the palm of the other hand. Bravo!

Sister Linda Karman, R.S.M., St. Elizabeth School, Pittsburgh, PA

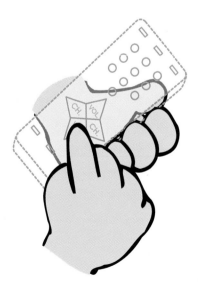

Remote Control

Empower children to display appropriate behavior with this tip. When it's necessary to ask your class to be quiet, suggest that they use their imaginary remote controls to turn down the volume of their voices. If a child is having difficulty, kindly offer him "fresh batteries" for his remote control.

Suzanne Costner—Preschool
Holy Trinity Preschool
Fayetteville, NC

A Rewarding Reptile

Use this add-a-bead snake to promote cooperation and other positive behaviors in your class. To make the snake, cut out a triangular head from tagboard. Add two wiggle eye stickers and a red felt tongue. Knot one end of a shoestring; then tape the knotted end to the back of the snake's head. As you observe positive behaviors in your class, add a large wooden bead to the snake. Challenge your students to earn a designated number of wooden beads daily to receive a class reward. At the end of the day, have the children count the beads. "Sssensational"!

Keitha-Lynn Stewart—Four-Year-Olds
Little Kids Day Care
Sissonville, WV

Reward Puzzle

All the pieces will fit together when you use this motivating reward system. Place a wooden puzzle frame without its pieces (12 pieces or less) on a table in the front of your room. Set the puzzle pieces next to the puzzle. Each time you catch a student doing something nice for someone else or you notice your class as a whole making an outstanding effort, add a puzzle piece to the puzzle. When the puzzle is completed, reward your little ones with an ice-cream party or video.

Wilma Droegemueller—Preschool/Gr. K
Zion Lutheran School
Mt. Pulaski, IL

Peaceful Puppet

Use a peaceful critter to help curb classroom noise and signal to youngsters that circle time is about to begin. Give a designated puppet a name such as Bashful Bunny, Hush Puppy, or Quiet Koala. Explain to your youngsters that this critter will not come to circle time until everyone is quiet. Your little ones will be eager to hear what special message the critter whispers, so circle time is likely to get off to a peaceful start.

Ann Gudowski—Pre/K and K
Turtle Rock Private School
Lake Forest, CA

Noise Control Game

Employ the domino effect to quiet classroom chatter before your students exit the room. Have the first student in line put his index finger to his lips and turn to the person behind him, showing this quiet signal. Then the second student in line puts his index finger to his lips and turns to the person behind him to show him the same quiet signal. In turn, each student continues the domino effect of the quiet signal until it reaches the last child in line. You won't even hear a whisper with this quiet chain reaction.

Sandy Simko, Brecht Elementary School, Lancaster, PA

Clap for Their Attention

When youngsters become distracted and talkative, use this technique to refocus their attention. Without speaking, clap a rhythm and encourage attentive youngsters to join in. Soon all of your little ones will be participating, and you'll have their undivided attention.

Marci Reimer-Haber
Ross Elementary
Nashville, TN

Good Behavior Buddy

Recognize positive classroom behavior with a cuddly, stuffed-animal buddy. Throughout the day, look for a student who is following directions, staying on task, or demonstrating positive behavior. Reward that child by placing a stuffed animal at his work area for a designated time; then continue to look for the next recipient. Keep a variety of stuffed animals on hand and rotate them seasonally. Students will delight in sharing their work areas with such snuggly critters.

Jeannie Ryan
Provident Heights School
Waco, TX

Brian

Good Behavior

Noise Level

To help your class keep the noise level down when working in groups, use this chart. Cue your class to what you expect the noise level to be by pointing to the appropriate picture on the chart. This will indicate to your youngsters how loud or soft their conversations should be. So whether the noise level should be as quiet as a mouse or roaring like a dragon, this chart is sure to be helpful.

Becky Wheeler
Woods Cross Elementary
Woods Cross, UT

Noise Level Chart		
0	No Talking	
1	Quiet Voices	
2	Normal Voices	
3	Outside Voices	

Star Sticks

Encourage good behavior by awarding star sticks. Each time appropriate behavior is noted, give a child a craft stick with a star on it to display in a visible place such as a behavior pocket. At the end of the day, congratulate each student who has a star stick. This illuminating idea is sure to be popular!

Becky A. Thompson
Willis Elementary School
Willis, VA

I Need Some Attention

Little ones who find themselves in new preschool settings may not know how to express their need for attention. Help them get the attention they need and deserve with decorated wristbands. Cut, assemble, and decorate some felt wristbands that fit your preschoolers. Place them in an accessible location. Encourage each youngster to wear a wristband whenever he needs a little extra attention. When you see a child wearing a wristband, be sure to touch base with him to find out what's on his mind and how you can improve his day.

Our Mission Statement

Class spirit and pride abound when youngsters help to author a mission statement for your classroom! To begin, lead youngsters in a discussion about why they come to school and what they hope to learn. Write their responses on the board. Next, condense that list into a sentence or two that everyone agrees upon. Write this newly created mission statement on chart paper. Then invite each child to sign the statement. Mount the signed statement on a sturdy colorful background and post it in a prominent place in your classroom. Periodically, read the statement aloud, encouraging children to join in the reading as they are able. Later, choose a different child each day to read/recite the statement during your morning group time.

Genie Merrer, Oldsmar, FL

October 26, 2003

Dear Jessica,
I hope you are having a good day at school. I just wanted to tell you how much I love you and also, how I love to hear you sing!

Love,
Dad

P.S. I can't wait for our music night together!

From Parents With Love

Doesn't everyone enjoy receiving a love letter every now and then? Your preschoolers will too—especially when the letters come from their own parents! Ask each parent to write a loving letter to her child, then drop it off at your school office or mail it in care of you. When you feel the time is right, don a construction paper postal hat and deliver the letters to the addressees. Encourage children to listen as you read their letters aloud. Then store the letters for later. Whenever a child comes down with the blues—or just because—read his letter again!

Latresa Bray
Townview Elementary
Dayton, OH

Self-Esteem

I Lost a Tooth!

Special Tees

Celebrate a birthday, a lost tooth, a student of the week, or some other favorite happening by making a whimsical T-shirt for the honoree to wear during the school day. Use fabric paints and any other embellishments of your choice to decorate a shirt for the designated occasion. (You may want to have two or three birthday shirts on hand, just in case!) Then invite the special student to wear this special tee on his special day. Afterwards, simply wash and dry the shirt for the next celebration. "Zip-a-tee-doo-dah, Zip-a-tee-ay! My, oh my, what a wonderful day!"

Laughing Scarf

Put each of your youngsters into a positive mood with a special laughing scarf. Select a bright scarf for this activity. Then have your youngsters decide what kind of laughing they will do. For instance, will the laughter be loud or quiet, high pitched or low pitched? Toss the scarf into the air, and encourage everyone to laugh until it touches the floor. But when it lands, specify that everyone is to become silent. Adapt this unusual activity to correspond with your thematic units. Instead of laughing, for example, students who are studying farm animals could moo, bray, or crow!

Jan Chastain, Holly Springs Elementary School, Pickens, SC

What Children Do Best

As we all know, every member of a family is important! This art activity will help each child understand his significance in his family. Read *What Mommies Do Best/What Daddies Do Best* by Laura Numeroff. After discussing the book, have students brainstorm other things that parents do. Record responses on a piece of chart paper. Then ask each child to think of one thing that he does best and have him draw a picture of the activity on a sheet of construction paper. Label students' drawings and then display them on a bulletin board with the title "What Children Do Best!" If desired, include a modified phrase similar to the one from the book's ending. What a masterpiece!

What Children Do Best!

Theo can feed the dog.

Alex can make his bed.

But best of all, children can give you lots and lots of love!

Alice can dust.

Jill can set the table.

Speeding Recovery

Being in a new preschool setting is unsettling for many students. Consequently every little problem may seem like a big deal. Be prepared to give extra doses of tender, loving care and spread warm feelings. Label a bottle of hand lotion "Hurt Cream." Whenever a child is hurt or in despair, apply a small amount of the hurt cream to the affected area or to his hands. The one-on-one attention the youngster gets along with your caring touch has a way of making the discomfort associated with bumps, bruises, and hurt feelings disappear.

Crowns

Treat your preschoolers like royalty. Use a bulletin board border to make a crown for each child. As you send him out the door wearing his crown, each youngster will stand a little taller.

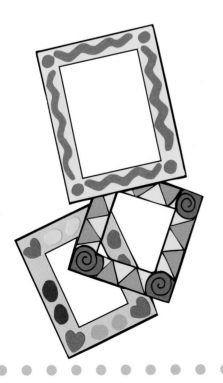

You Ought to Be in Pictures

Give each of your students an ongoing opportunity to be the center of attention by exhibiting photographs of the children's choice. Caption a bulletin board "Say Cheese!" Then have students paint cardboard frames, cut to fit the most common size of prints that you get. Encourage students to bring photos from home, or select classroom-made pictures to frame. Whenever a student is ready to fill his frame or change the picture, offer him assistance. Tape the picture to the back of the opening and have the student attach the picture to the board. As pictures are removed from the board, ask the students' permission to add them to a class photo album. Allow each student to take the photo album home from time to time.

Game Management

Keep track of the many games your youngsters complete with this motivating, star-studded idea. Store your manipulative games in a box and place the box on a table. Supply each child with an index card programmed with circles labeled to correspond with the games. Each time a student completes a game from the box, put a star in the corresponding circle and write the date above it. Encourage each student to complete as many games as he wishes in the allotted time. When a child gets all of his circles starred, provide him with a new card; then reward him with a treat or star sticker.

Lori O'Malley
Dingman Delaware Elementary School
Dingmans Ferry, PA

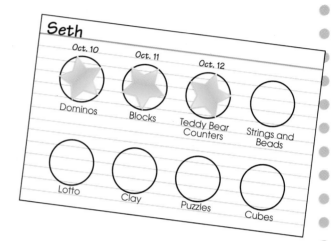

Placemat Space

Your space or mine? Use placemats to define individual work spaces for your little ones. Give each child her own placemat when working with play dough or manipulatives. Because each child can easily see her work area, disputes over materials are prevented. Whose is that? Just look at your mat!

Teresa Hanak, Fenton Preschool, Fenton, MI

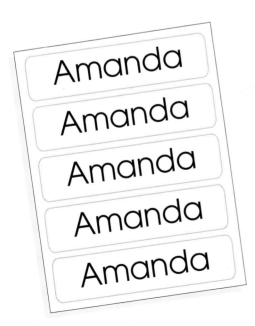

"A-peel-ing" Names

Here's a timesaving tip to help youngsters label their own work. For each child, have an adult volunteer program a sheet of computer labels. Instruct each child to keep his labeled sheet in his supply box or cubby. When the child finishes a piece of work, he peels a label from the sheet and attaches it to his work. As an incentive, have blank labels ready for children who are primed to program them with their names themselves.

Eleanor Jean Willits—PreK
Allan Elementary School
Austin, TX

Communication

Contents

Parents

Make Contact

Stick with your effort to make contact with parents with this terrific tip. Cut solid-colored Con-Tact paper into note-size geometric shapes. (Or use a die-cutter machine to cut seasonal and thematic shapes out of the paper.) The next time you need to send a reminder home with a child or pass on a word of praise about an accomplishment, use a permanent marker to jot a note onto one of the cutouts. Remove the backing and then press the note onto the child's clothing. These colorful reminders are sure to get parents' attention!

Shoshanna Katz—Two- to Five-Year-Olds, Special Education
Marathon Childhood Center Forest Hills West
Middle Village, NY

Reminder: Pumpkin patch trip tomorrow!

Book orders due on Friday.

1. Attendance Policy
2. Class Rules
3. Daily Snack Schedule
4. Field Trips

Agenda Strips

Here's a good organizational method to try if you're going to be talking to parents as a group about different aspects of kindergarten or preschool. Write each topic on a sentence strip and attach these to your chalkboard. Not only can you see at a glance which topics you still need to mention, but parents who have to slip out early can also see which things they'll need to inquire about later.

Cathy Gressley, Brown Elementary School
St. Joseph, MI

A Nifty Notebook

Organize notes from parents with manila envelopes and a binder. To make a book of parent correspondence, label each of several manila envelopes with a different student's name. Then bind the envelopes together in a spiral binding or a three-ring binder. When you receive a note from a parent, store it in the corresponding envelope. This system is a great way to keep all of your correspondence in one place.

Monica D. Phillips—Pre/K, Jefferson Elementary, Houston, TX

Jenn

Artsy Envelopes

Share youngsters' artwork with these child-decorated envelopes! Attach blank address labels to a large supply of white envelopes; then place them in your writing center. Invite youngsters to use crayons or water-based markers to decorate the envelopes without coloring the labels. Each time you send home a parent note, just place it inside a decorated envelope. Say, that's an artsy home-school connection right at your fingertips!

Teresa Pearsall—Preschool
Step by Step Childcare Center
Williamston, NC

Message in a Bottle

Send special notes home in this eye-catching container! To make a message bottle, cover a clean, empty Pringles can with colorful Con-Tact paper. Write a note similar to the one shown and then glue it to the outside of the container. When a child has had a good day, place a positive note to parents inside the container. Then add a special treat for the child to enjoy at home.

Glenda Prichard—Three-Year-Olds and Pre-K
First Baptist Preschool
Athens, TN

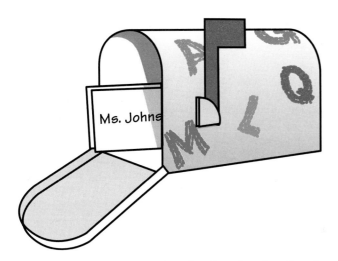

A Note for Teacher—in the Mail!

Need to make sure parents' notes to you get delivered? Try this attractive idea! Use alphabet sponges and bright paints to decorate a mailbox. Then put it in your classroom near the area where students keep their coats and belongings. As students unpack, remind them to put any notes from home in the mail to you. Also request that they put up the flag on the mailbox to show you that you've got mail. What a first-class tip!

Sally Thigpen, Franklinton Primary School, Franklinton, LA

Answering Machine Memos

Here's a system that keeps parents up-to-date on current school information, promotes events, and encourages parents to leave messages for teachers—all at everyone's convenience! Each week record a message on your school's answering machine that includes the desired information and requests that parents ask questions or leave messages for specific teachers. Hello! Thank you for calling!

Janice Denney—Preschool
Iola Preschool for Exceptional Children
Iola, KS

Family of the Week

To foster the home-school connection, feature a different child's family each week! At the beginning of school, ask parents to sign up for the week that they would like to be featured. Then send a reminder note home to each family prior to its designated week. In this note, request that the child share family pictures on the first day of the week. Then suggest additional ways the family can participate in its featured week, such as having a family member visit for a morning, bringing the family pet to school, sending a favorite family snack to school, reading the daily story, preparing a video introducing the child's family, and more. You may even choose to send a certificate home after a family's week, recognizing them for strengthening the home-school connection!

Betsy Fuhrmann—Pre-K
Dodds-Early Start Program
Springfield, IL

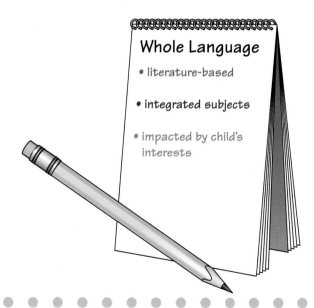

Charting Your Course

If you plan to take a few minutes to speak to your parents as a group, consider this flip-chart organizational method. Use a different sheet of chart paper for each topic that you plan to discuss. Use alternating colors of markers to note the key points beneath each topic. For fun, write an assignment for parents on the last chart page. Ask each of them to write a 500-word essay on what her child will learn in kindergarten. When the nervous giggles die down, explain that, of course, you are kidding.

Jessica Shuler
Coconut Creek Elementary
Coconut Creek, FL

It Goes Both Ways

These folders make it easy for information to travel both ways—home and back to school again. Personalize the outside of a two-pocket folder for each child. Invite each child to use markers or stickers to decorate his folder. Encourage parents to check the folders daily for important messages, words of praise, behavior reports, and more. Ensure parents that you'll be checking the folders daily as well for any messages parents may need to send to you.

Barbara Morganweck—Preschool, Handicapped
Downe Township School, Newport, NJ

Parent Pockets

Here's an idea to ensure that important papers get from school to home—and back again! For each child, label a large string-tie envelope with his name and class. Encourage each child to decorate his envelope; then laminate the envelopes. Cut along each envelope's flap with an X-acto knife. Presto! Parent Pockets are a practical, portable, water-resistant means of transporting communications between home and school.

Karin Thompson, Conley School, Bethlehem Township, NJ

Photo Craze

Next year's students and parents will look forward to the preschool year after thumbing through this memorable album. As you collect photos this year, set aside a few each month that depict typical classroom events. At the end of the year, arrange all the photos in an album. During your visitations of incoming preschoolers, place the album beneath a sign that reads "Take a Look at This Book!" Encourage children and parents to get a feel for what they can expect in the coming year by looking through this special album.

Marlene Baker
Mars Hill Bible School
Florence, AL

Parents

Stick It or Stamp It

Preparing classroom newsletters and calendars will be easy with this nifty idea. Instead of clipping, saving, reducing, enlarging, gluing, and taping clip art, use rubber stamps and stickers. They fit in small spaces, copy well, and are readily available. With the tremendous selection on the market, you're sure to find just what you need. So stick it or stamp it!

Beth Lemke—PreK
Heights Head Start
Coon Rapids, MN

It's in There!

Here's a resource your parents will love! Type up all of those things that parents will eventually need or want to know about. Some of the things you might prepare include a class schedule, a list of themes for the year, planned field trips, students' names, parents' names and phone numbers, a birthday list, party guidelines, and a volunteer sign-up sheet. Punch holes in all of the pages except the volunteer form, which you'll want parents to return. Collate the hole-punched pages and fasten them into colorful, inexpensive folders along with a loose copy of the volunteer form. Later—when volunteers have been assigned to specific tasks—you can send a listing of assignments to parents to be added to the folder. Since all of the important information is in one place, parents seldom have to call and inquire about small details.

Debbie Monts de Oca—Preschool
St. Paul's Episcopal School, Winter Haven, FL

Date Stamp

Do you like to show parents the progress in their children's work? Try this timesaving tip. As a child finishes a paper or project, stamp the date on it with a date stamp. Now his work can easily be chronologically organized, and a parent can see his child's progress at a glance.

Debi Myer, Lincoln School, Ottawa, IL

Parents Are Teachers Too!

You'll have more and more participating teachers with this motivating idea. Begin by inviting a parent to share a hobby, career, craft, talent, or story with your little ones. Take several candid photos of each parent as she interacts with your students. Place these photos in a resealable plastic bag that has been stapled to the inside of a file folder. Inside the folder, glue a class-dictated letter explaining what the parent shared with the class, and include some anecdotal remarks. Glue a library pocket on the back so students can check out the folders to take home and share with their parents. Once these folders start traveling to each child's home, other parents will see how fun and easy it is to volunteer. (This also serves as a great recruiting device for parents or other volunteers who have special skills or experiences but wouldn't even consider the skills worthy of sharing without your prompting!)

Joan Piela, Woodrow Wilson #5, Garfield, NJ

Mr. Mayworth can play the guitar. He is called a musician, but he works on telephones too. He sang a song about a frog. It was really funny.

Mrs. Crane can draw a picture of anything you can think of! She is an artist. Mrs. Crane drew every animal we could say in the alphabet. She is Jackson's mom.

PTA Reminders

It's easy for parents to forget about a PTA meeting, even though reminders are sent home ahead of time. One way to increase parent participation is to call each child's home to personally invite the parents. Another last-minute reminder can be delivered on the day of the meeting. Before each student leaves for the day, loosely tie a ribbon around one of his fingers. Explain that the ribbon is a reminder to him to remind his parents that this is PTA day.

Patt Hall, Babson Park Elementary, Lake Wales, FL

Circle Time

Picture This

When making home visits, keep in mind that many parents may be unable to visit your classroom during school hours. To make the descriptions of your class activities clear, take along photos. In advance of your home visits, take pictures of your classroom activities, making sure to get each child in one or more shots. Have double prints made of the pictures. Organize the first set of pictures in an album. While you are visiting a parent, have her look at pictures that relate to the information you are sharing. Then invite her to choose pictures that include her child to keep from the second set of prints.

Janis Woods—Four-Year-Olds, Ridgeland Elementary
Ridgeland, SC

Parents

My Buddy and Me

On his first day in your class, send a recent enrollee home with a special memento of the occasion. Using a Polaroid camera, photograph the new student engaged in an activity with a buddy. This photograph is sure to give the newcomer and his parents a great deal of pleasure as they discuss the events of the child's first day.

Here's My Card

Provide parents with all the information they need to contact you with these business cards that double as refrigerator magnets. Using a computer program, design a business card, similar to the one shown, that contains your phone numbers and email address. Print the cards on card stock so that you have one for each family; then laminate them. Cut the cards apart; then attach a piece of magnetic tape to the back of each one. When it is displayed on the refrigerator, each card makes a quick reference and a super way to display a child's work too!

Emily R. Wargel—PreK
Louisville Deaf Oral School, Louisville, KY

Emily Wargel
Louisville Deaf Oral School
Work: 555-1234
Home: 555-5678
Email: teacheremily@thesite.com

Home-School Connection

Looking for new ways to strengthen the home-school connection? Then try this fun idea to help families reinforce concepts taught in preschool. At the beginning of each week, invite each child's family to work with her to complete a short list of hands-on activities. Children will enjoy the family interaction, parents will appreciate new ways to help their child, and you'll notice the extra skill reinforcement. Everyone benefits from a strong home-school connection!

Jane Chastain, Holly Springs Elementary School, Pickens, SC

At-Home Fun Work
1. Count all the forks.
   Count all the spoons.
   Which set has more?
2. Find 10 blue items.
3. Find 3 round items.

We Left Our Pad

Use this "toad-ally" clever idea, and classroom visitors who find your room empty will know where to look for your group. Prepare a frog cutout and six green lily pad cutouts; then mount the lily pads on poster board. Label each lily pad with a specific destination. Laminate the pieces and mount them outside your classroom door, clipping the frog cutout to the poster with a clothespin. Each day, have a classroom helper move the frog as necessary to indicate the location of your group.

Bev Wirt
Desert Valley School
Glendale, AZ

Put a Face With the Name

Chances are, many parents want to put faces with the names that their children have been mentioning during the first few days of school. Help with that goal by providing a copy of a page with a picture of every student.

Patricia Dempsey
School of the Transfiguration
Corona, NY

Wishing Well

Need items for your classroom? Make a wish at the wishing well! Mount a wishing well design onto a background; then surround it with self-adhesive notes labeled with your requests. Parents simply take off a note and then send the requested item(s) to school. Prepare this display for an open house or anytime to let parents know of your needs all through the year.

Lucia Roney, Orange Park, FL

Parents

The Giving Tree

Draw a tree outline on your chalkboard. On the foliage, attach small apple cutouts, each of which bears the name of an item or items you need for classroom use. For instance, you might list paper plates, baby food jars, oatmeal boxes, margarine tubs, lunch sacks, markers, pom-poms, and so forth. Write a note on the board explaining that any parent who is willing to donate an indicated item should take the corresponding apple cutout and send the item to school at her convenience.

Christy Owens
West Alexandria Elementary, West Alexandria, OH

Sentiments

When you're corresponding with parents for the final time during this school year, include this poem to convey your sentiments.

Great Expectations

It's time to say goodbye.
Our year has come to an end.
I've made more cherished memories
And many more new friends.

I've watched your children learn and grow
And change from day to day.
I hope that all the things we've done
Have helped in some small way.

So it's with happy memories
I send them out the door,
With great hope and expectations
For what next year holds in store.

Maria Cuellar-Munson, Garland, TX

Topic Trackers

Turn parents and children into topic trackers by asking them to help locate items for upcoming themes or topics. You can do this in your weekly newsletter or use the parent note on page 72. To use the reproducible, make one copy; then write in the topic and add a deadline for bringing the items to school. Then make a class supply. Parents and children instantly become involved in your school topics. Now that's the track of purposeful parent involvement!

Judy Clifford
Central Elementary, Point Pleasant, WV

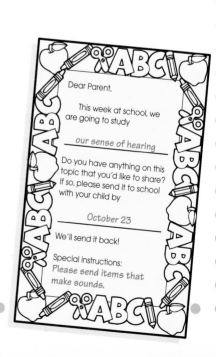

Let's Get It Home!

Is it difficult for your preschoolers to get important papers home? Try this unique solution! For each child, provide an empty potato chip can with a plastic lid. Cover the cans with colored construction paper. Use a permanent marker to personalize each one with a child's name, school, and teacher name. Then let students decorate their cans using a variety of art materials. When important papers need to go home, simply roll them up and place them in the appropriate cans. Put the lids on to keep the papers safely inside.

Anna N. Clemons—Preschool
LBJ Elementary
Jackson, KY

A Surprise in the Mailbox

Before school begins, address a couple of postcards for each of your students. Stamp the postcards and tuck them away for later use. Whenever you observe something that is especially delightful about a particular child, jot a note on a postcard labeled with his name. Mail the postcard. When it arrives at his home, everyone will be delighted that you took the time to comment.

Ask Me Where I Worked Today

Parents are sure to appreciate this idea, which helps them ask their children meaningful questions about the school day and reminds them of the learning benefits of play. To implement this tip, draw a simple diagram of your classroom, noting all of your centers. On a separate page, list each of your centers and the benefits of play there. For each child, duplicate the diagram and the list on opposite sides of a colorful sheet of paper. Laminate the sheets.

Each day, use a wipe-off marker to indicate on a child's sheet those centers at which he played. Then have the child take the sheet home to share with a parent. "I worked at sand today and built a castle!"

Betsy Fuhrmann—PreK, Dodds Early Start, Springfield, IL

Parents

Oct. 4

Mrs. Dominguez,
Please send Cassie's permission slip to school by Friday.

Ms. Secor

Cassie

A Noteworthy Idea

Even with the best of plans, drop-off times and pickup times can be hectic. Use this communication idea to make sure parents know you value their thoughts and concerns. Write each child's name on her own small spiral notepad. Then store each child's notepad in her cubby. Encourage parents to write messages to you in the notebooks. Likewise, when necessary write the parent a message, making sure the child takes her notepad home with her that day.

Lori Secor—PreK, Children's Corner Daycare, Albany, NY

Friday Folders

To help make communication with parents a simple task, use Friday folders. Supply each child with a personalized two-pocket folder. Each Friday place newsletters, calendars (highlighting special events and dates), rewards, and memos in the folders; then have each child take his folder home. Encourage each youngster to return his folder on Monday so it can be reused the next week. Parents will love getting their weekly special deliveries and being kept up on all the scoops.

Reneé Martin, Westwood Hills Elementary School, Waynesboro, VA

And the Survey Says...

Everybody puts his two cents in with this idea, which incorporates beginning keyboarding skills, parent involvement, math, and a whole lot more! First, send home a survey with several appropriate questions, such as "What do you like best about school?" or "What is your favorite flavor of ice cream?" Ask each parent to interview her child, record his dictation, and return the survey to school. Set up a computer page to record all the incoming information. Position the cursor for each child (or have a volunteer do this); then have each child type his own name. If your survey answers lend themselves to graphing, plug that information into a computer program that makes graphs. Give each child a copy of the resulting graph; then have him color each bar a different color. Staple each graph to a copy of the next newsletter; then send it home. Each time you send home a survey, more and more parents will participate because they will want to see their children's names in the news!

Cindy Daoust, Johnson Elementary, Franklin, TN

Our Favorite Things At School	Our Favorite Ice-Cream Flavors
Adam—the playground	Chelsea—chocolate
Cody—stuff with numbers, like math	David—just vanilla
Jackson—art	Kelly—chocolate chip
Missy—I like to read.	Ali—strawberry
Callie—I like all of the stuff!	Kristen—chocolate
Ali—music time	Michael—fudge ripple
David—circle time	Adam—vanilla with sprinkles
Michael—lunchtime	Cody—chocolate
Kristen—when we read books together	Jackson—vanilla
	Missy—vanilla

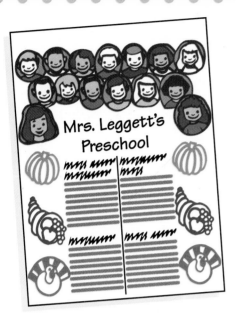

Headline News

Your students literally make headlines with this nifty newsletter idea. Arrange your students' school photos along the top of a sheet of unlined paper. Add a title; then photocopy a supply of the page. Use one of these pages as your original each time you create a classroom newsletter. If desired, stamp different seasonal prints along the border of each new newsletter. Write your weekly news on the page; then photocopy a class supply. Your youngsters' cheerful faces will entice their families to read all about it!

Susan Gaffney
Marie Duffy Elementary School
Wharton, NJ

A Picture Is Worth...

To help parents better understand how their children are learning at school, take some time to create this photo album of your classroom activities and centers. Over a period of time, take pictures of children doing a variety of activities, such as playing in centers, participating in group activities, and taking part in such routines as washing hands or napping. Arrange the pictures in an album along with brief explanations. Invite each child, in turn, to take the book home; then put it in your reading area for students to look at and discuss. Pictures really are worth a thousand words!

Cindy Lawson—Toddler to PreK, Shell Lake, WI

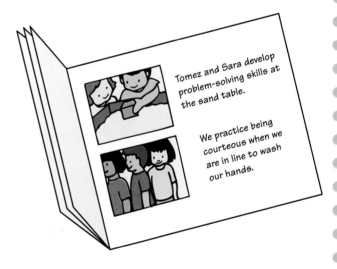

Tomez and Sara develop problem-solving skills at the sand table.

We practice being courteous when we are in line to wash our hands.

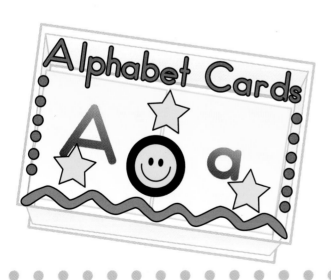

Surprise Boxes

Looking for a clever way to send home learning activities to help parents reinforce basic skills? Try clear plastic videocassette boxes! Use dimensional fabric paint and stickers to decorate the outside of a number of empty boxes. Then fill each box with items such as alphabet flash cards, manipulatives and a card programmed with activity suggestions, or puzzle pieces. Children will enjoy taking the goodies home, and parents will appreciate the learning opportunities provided.

Amy Drake, Fort Wayne, IN

Parents

Party Reminders for Parents

Invite parents to participate in your holiday parties with this display. In advance, cut out pairs of seasonal shapes. Label each pair with a different item needed for your party and the date on which you need it. Then use pushpins to mount the pairs together on a bulletin board that is visible and accessible to parents. Add a large note similar to the one shown and then staple a decorated lunch bag to the board. A few days before your party, check the board to see what items parents will be sending. Ah, planning a party has never been so easy!

Angie Jenkins—Two-Year-Olds, Love to Learn
Knoxville, TN

Let's Have a Party!

cups 2/14

cupcakes 2/14

punch 2/14

napkins 2/14

plates 2/14

Dear Parents,
   If you would like to help with our Valentine's Day party, please choose an item listed on a pair of hearts. Write your name on one heart and place it in the bag. Keep the other heart as a reminder. Send the item to school on or before the date listed.
   Thank you!

Preschool's Greatest Hits

What better way to share youngsters' favorite tunes than with this tape of chart toppers? Tape-record your youngsters singing their favorite songs; then duplicate the tape for parents. Not only is this a great way to share the tunes with families, but it also makes a terrific addition to field trip kits for parent drivers. Just pack a copy of the tape along with a destination map and emergency numbers for each driver. Say, does anybody know "The Wheels on the Bus"?

Teresa Pugmire—PreK, Calvin Smith Elementary, Salt Lake City, UT

Weekly News

Keep 'em Posted

Keep parents posted with a bulletin board provided just for them. Arrange a display area near your school or classroom entrance. Cut one or more pocket folders in half; then staple the halves to your display. Make copies of such items as your weekly newsletter, important forms, or articles to store in the pockets. Encourage parents to check the display often, taking copies of the pages that are of interest to them. To make sure the display remains eye-catching, add pictures of children at the school.

Melissa Batten—Two- and Three-Year-Olds, Sumter, SC

All About You!

You've all had those precious little ones that respond with shock when they learn that teachers actually leave the school building in the evenings and do ordinary things, such as shop in grocery stores, walk their dogs, or eat at restaurants. Create an all-about-you book to help your new batch of preschoolers get to know you and feel more comfortable in your classroom. In advance, gather a collection of photos that show you in settings or situations that children are likely to find interesting, such as with your family, friends, pets, or on a vacation. Arrange and mount the photos on sheets of construction paper. Then add simple captions for each picture. Laminate the pages; then bind them together behind a laminated cover. Display this book during meet-the-teacher times and the first few days of school. This book will be in high demand!

Angela Van Beveren
Alvin, TX

Memory Jogger

Keep track of important reminders with this simple idea. Type a list of all the children in your class. Make several copies. Laminate one copy and post it near your door. Use a dry-erase marker to jot down notes about transportation, medications, or other reminders next to children's names. Erase the notes at the end of each day and the list will be ready to use again. You'll find many uses for the other copies of the list, such as keeping track of which children have brought in permission slips for a field trip.

Sally Greiner—Early Childhood Special Education
Metzenbaum School, Chesterland, OH

End-of-the-Day Reminder

Do you sometimes forget things you should remind students of at the end of the day? If so, then write "Please Remember" at the top of a sheet of poster board. Color, decorate, and laminate the poster. Attach a length of string to a corner, and tie a wipe-off marker to the end of the string. Tape the poster to the inside of your classroom door. During the day, as you think of things that students will need to be reminded of, write them on the poster with the wipe-off marker. At the end of the day, refer to the "Please Remember" reminder before sending students home.

Jeanette N. Allen—Special Education
Cottonwood, AZ

Early-Learner's Clock

You'll save lots of time answering those "How long till…" questions with this idea that uses picture cues to help children learn concepts of time. Cut out a paper collar for your clock as shown; then tape it on the wall. Beside each of the clock's numerals, attach a different sticker to the collar. Attach a strip of colored paper to the minute hand. Now when a child asks "How long till…," refer to the colored minute hand and the sticker beside the appropriate clock numeral. For example, you might say, "When the green hand points to the heart."

Carole Smith—Head Start
Mango Elementary
Seffner, FL

The Happy Stick

When you find yourself with a minute or two to spare, pass around the happy stick. Not only will this activity help little ones learn to accentuate the positive, but you'll also get some insight into the things that are happening in their lives. Prepare for this activity ahead of time by using decorative fabric paints to draw a smiling expression on a red felt heart. Then use craft glue to attach the heart to a wide craft stick or tongue depressor. When the opportunity arises, seat youngsters in a circle. Then encourage the children to pass the happy stick around. Each time the stick is passed to another person, that child tells something that made her happy that day. Be sure to take a turn yourself, since everyone will want to hear your positive comments as well. Once you've used this five-minute filler, your youngsters will ask for it again and again.

Mary Mierow—Preschool
Holy Cross Lutheran Preschool
Prior Lake, MN

Dear Boys and Girls

Encourage your youngsters to have a great day—even while you're temporarily absent! Along with all the other information that you leave for your substitute, include a letter to your youngsters that is similar to the one shown. After the letter, list each child's name and leave a space for glowing comments from the substitute. What child could pass up this invitation to shine? Upon returning, read the comments aloud to the group to reinforce their positive behaviors. Remember to place a revised letter with your other substitute materials—just in case there's a next time!

Ann Rowe
Western Hills Elementary
Omaha, NE

Dear Boys And Girls,

I'm sorry that I won't see you today. I don't want to miss out on all the fun. Please have your substitute teacher write me sentences telling me all the good things you did for her and for your friends today. I know you will have a good day because you are the best class ever!

Mrs. Rowe

Jackson _____
Amy _____
Spencer _____
Tara _____
Cindy _____
Randall _____
Jennifer _____
Samuel _____
Carla _____

Magic Circle

Use a circle of yarn as a "magic circle" to establish a one-on-one working relationship with individual students. During your youngsters' free-time activities, place a circle of yarn on a rug; then sit inside the magic circle with a designated student. Use this time to review a specific skill, read aloud a book, or chat with your student. Choose a different child each day for the magic circle. Your little ones will love the idea of receiving such special attention.

Stephanie Larson—Speech-Language Pathologist, Iola, KS

Ms. Lucy Proia
21A Guyer Street
High Point, NC 24856

Luke Bolka
14 S

Dear Luke
I am very excited about our first day of school. I'm looking forward to having you in my classroom. We will have lots of fun and we'll learn many new things this year.
Please wear your school bus nametag when you come to school on the first day. I have some special activities planned!
See you soon! Ms. Proia

Luke

Can't Wait to See You!

Calm those first-day jitters and create a sense of positive anticipation by letting your new class know that you are thinking about them. A week or two before school begins send a welcome-to-school pack to each child. Personalize a note similar to the one shown for each student. Place each note in a manila envelope along with a personalized nametag and a picture of yourself. This little contact will do big things to create a sense of welcome and warmth for your new arrivals.

Stephanie Larson—Speech-Language Pathologist

Substitutes

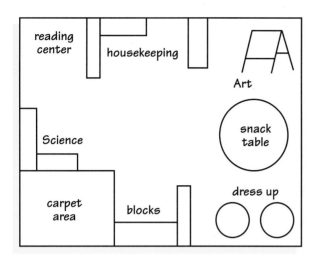

Substitute's Map
Help your substitute become familiar with your room by providing her with a map. In advance, draw a map of your classroom and label the map to include areas such as centers, seating arrangements, and the location of supplies. Duplicate several copies of the map. The next time you are preparing plans for a substitute, be sure to include your classroom map.

Theresa Lux—PreK
Pumpkin Patch Nursery School Centers, Inc.
Guilderland, NY

Getting Feedback
Along with the other materials that you leave for the substitute teacher, include a four- or five-sentence questionnaire. On the questionnaire, ask her: What things did you need but never find? What things did I neglect to inform you of that you really needed to know? Which youngsters were the most helpful? What other problems or questions did you encounter? Take this feedback into consideration as you plan for your next substitute teacher.

Kathleen Ryan
Scio Central School
Scio, NY

Handle With Care
Use this system and you'll never have to worry about a substitute who's unaware of your youngsters with special needs. On a copy of your attendance sheet or enrollment list, place a tiny sticker by the name of each youngster who needs special attention due to concerns such as medication, physical limitations, or custody restrictions. Include brief notes to inform the substitute of the necessary steps or precautions. Display this list prominently with the substitute's other materials.

Diane Swetz
Loyalhanna Elementary School
Derry, PA

	12/14	12/15	12/16	12/17	12/18	
⊘ Dana Adams	✓	✓				
Todd Beck	✓	✓				
Ben Belangia	✓	✓				
⊘ Dion Drust		✓				
Davis Fillingame	✓	✓				
Charley Gaulden		✓				
Chihiro Kase	✓	✓				
Jose Maturino	✓	✓				

Goodie Box

Treat your substitute teacher like royalty. When you know you'll have a substitute, fill a small decorative box with an assortment of mints, tea bags, hot chocolate mixes, or instant coffees. Include a brief note of thanks for her efforts. Then place the box on top of her lesson plans. Don't you wish you could be there to see her expression?

Nancy Dunaway
Hughes Elementary
Forrest City, AR

Have One on Me!

Whether you keep your substitute teacher supplies in a folder or a box, this little kindness is sure to make someone's day. On a colorful sheet of paper, tape enough coins for a soft drink. On the same sheet, jot a note saying, "Thanks for all your help. Have a soda on me!" It's a small way to set a pleasant tone for your substitute teacher's day.

Gayle Colburn, Livingston Primary School, Livingston, TX

Sub Survival Kit

We all know that it's a jungle out there! Substitute teachers are on the firing lines every day, never knowing what challenge may lurk just ahead. Delight and pamper your next substitute with this too-good-to-be-true survival kit. Recycle an old first aid kit by cleaning and painting it. Then use a paint pen to label it "Substitute Survival Kit." Make photocopied reductions of important classroom information; then cut out and glue the reduced information to colorful (5" x 8") index cards. Write each of the sentences that follow on an additional card and attach the indicated goodie. Place the goodie cards in the kit on top of the information cards. Now you know she'll survive!

Card 1—To help you through this day, I have compiled some general information and some essential supplies. Help yourself!
Card 2—Avoid midmorning rumblings by nibbling on this candy bar. A little chocolate never hurt anyone. *Attach a candy bar.*
Card 3—Thirsty? Use this change to have a soda on me! You deserve it! *Tape on the exact change.*
Card 4—If you are fortunate enough to share one of those precious preschool moments that makes you laugh until you cry, say you got something in your eye and use these tissues. *Attach a small packet of tissues.*
Card 5—If the newness of your assignment results in a tension headache, help yourself to this remedy. *Attach a packet of pain reliever.*
Card 6—Strained voice a problem? Help yourself to some cough drops. *Attach a small packet of cough drops.*
Card 7—At day's end, slip into this bubble bath. Soak your cares away! *Attach a packet of bubble bath.*

Jan Utesch, Remsen-Union Elkementary School, Remsen, IA

Volunteers

Clever Thank-Yous

Show gratitude with one of these clever thank-you notes. Write a message in a blank notecard that relates to the name of a particular candy, gum, or item such as those listed below. Then tape one or two of the actual treats to the message inside the card. This little added extra is sure to make a classroom helper feel special!

Thanks for the extra help! (Wrigley's Extra gum)
You're a star! (Starburst fruit chews)
Thanks a mint! (mint candy)
You're worth your weight in gold! (gold foil-wrapped chocolate coins)
Hugs and kisses from our class! (Hershey's Hugs and Hershey's Kisses candies)
You're a lifesaver! (Life Savers candies)

Shelly Fales
Whittemore-Prescott Early Childhood Center
Whittemore, MI

Seeds of Learning

Your volunteers help cultivate learning in your classroom; now show thanks with these special potted plants. Purchase a medium to large terra-cotta flowerpot for each person. Have students use permanent markers to sign and decorate each pot; then insert a beautiful flower or plant. Include a note that reads "You have helped us grow! Thank you!"

Becca Hughes
Wisconsin Conservatory of Lifelong Learning
Milwaukee, WI

Flowerful Thanks!

This child-made flower arrangement is the perfect thank-you gift for classroom volunteers or special helpers. To make one, you'll need a clean terra-cotta flowerpot (or substitute a decorated shoebox if desired). Cut a piece of floral foam to fit the bottom of the pot. Have each child make a flower stem by painting a craft stick green. When the paint is dry, have him write his name on the stem. Next, have him cut out petals and leaves from construction paper or craft foam. Then instruct him to glue the pieces to the stem. Invite each child to insert his flower into the pot. Finally, tuck in a little class-made card thanking the volunteer for her time. Thanks a whole bunch!

Sara Wendahl, St. Mary's School, Waukesha, WI

How Can I Help?

Many fortunate teachers have been asked by parents, "How can I help?" Use volunteer cards to answer that question and to encourage parents to help in ways that are most convenient for them. When you need a volunteer, identically label two index cards with "Volunteer Card" and the specific request. Clip the cards together; then post them on a parent bulletin board in a highly visible area, such as the class entrance. To volunteer for a task, a parent selects a pair of cards, then pulls them apart. She keeps one card as a reminder. Then she writes her name on the second card and gives it to you for your records.

Cynthia J. Stefanick—PreK, Lajes Elementary School
Terceira, Portuguese Azores

Volunteer Card

Trace and cut out 20 bear shapes by Nov. 1.

An Umbrella of Gratitude

This personalized umbrella keeps your valuable volunteers out of the weather. For each gift, purchase a large solid-colored umbrella from a local discount store. Open the umbrella and place it on a table along with a supply of fabric markers. Have each youngster use the markers to draw a self-portrait and then sign his name. After all students have personalized the umbrella, present it to your volunteer along with a note that reads, "Whatever the weather, we think you shine! Thank you for helping our class."

Linda Doser
The Learning Center
Dickeyville, WI

Volunteers

Teatime!

Thank volunteers for their help throughout the year with these sun-tea jars. To make a gift, purchase a one-gallon sun-tea jar and a box of tea bags. Wrap the box in yellow tissue paper and place it in the jar. Then tie a ribbon around the neck of the jar and attach a note that reads "You've brightened our year! We appreciate your help!" The volunteers will beam!

Lana Pratt
Northwood Elementary
San Antonio, TX

A Round of Applause

Recognize each volunteer's hard work with this simple one-of-a-kind poster. Begin by writing the poem shown on a large sheet of paper. Then glue the paper to the center of a sheet of poster board. Have each child dip her hand in paint and make a print on the poster board near the edge. After the paint dries, have each youngster use a permanent marker to sign her handprint. As a group, present the poster to your very deserving volunteer.

Shannon Hynes
St. Jude Catholic School
Boca Raton, FL

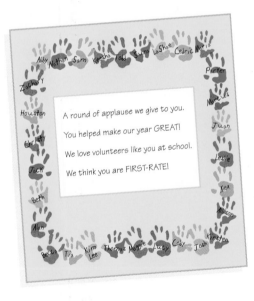

A round of applause we give to you.
You helped make our year GREAT!
We love volunteers like you at school.
We think you are FIRST-RATE!

It's in the Mail

This special delivery is sure to bring a smile to your volunteers' faces. To begin, display an appropriate message on the changeable information board of your school's sign, such as "[Volunteer's name] is a great volunteer! We appreciate your help!" or "Volunteers at [name of your school] are the best!" (If your school doesn't have a sign of this sort, display the message on a bulletin board.) For each volunteer, take a photograph of your youngsters standing around the message. Place each photo in an inexpensive frame and then mail it to a volunteer in a padded envelope. What a surprise!

Dianne R. Anderson
Hickerson Elementary
Tullahoma, TN